RESEARCH ON REFLECTIVE PRACTICE IN TESOL

In this comprehensive and detailed analysis of recent research on encouraging reflective practices in TESOL, Farrell demonstrates how this practice has been embraced within TESOL and how it continues to impact the field. Examining a vast array of studies through his own framework for reflecting on practice, Farrell's analysis comprises not only the intellectual and cognitive but also the spiritual, moral, and emotional aspects of reflection. Reflection questions at the end of each chapter provide a jumping-off point for researchers, scholars, and teachers to further consider and reflect on the future of the field. Providing a holistic picture of reflection, this book is an original compendium of essential research on philosophy and principles, instruments used in studies, and theory and practice.

Thomas S.C. Farrell is Professor of Applied Linguistics at Brock University, Canada.

ESL & APPLIED LINGUISTICS PROFESSIONAL SERIES

Series Editor: Eli Hinkel

Researching Second Language Classrooms
McKay

CALL Research Perspectives
Egbert/Petrie, Eds.

Reclaiming the Local in Language Policy and Practice
Canagarajah, Ed.

Language Minority Students in American Schools: An Education in English
Adamson

New Perspectives on CALL for Second Language Classrooms
Fotos/Browne, Eds.

Teaching Academic ESL Writing: Practical Techniques in Vocabulary and Grammar
Hinkel

New Perspectives on Grammar Teaching in Second Language Classrooms
Hinkel/Fotos, Eds.

Second Language Writers' Text: Linguistic and Rhetorical Features
Hinkel

For more information on this series visit: www.routledge.com/education for additional information on titles in the ESL & Applied Linguistics Professional Series

RESEARCH ON REFLECTIVE PRACTICE IN TESOL

Thomas S.C. Farrell

Routledge
Taylor & Francis Group

NEW YORK AND LONDON

First published 2018
by Routledge
711 Third Avenue, New York, NY 10017

and by Routledge
2 Park Square, Milton Park, Abingdon, Oxon OX14 4RN

Routledge is an imprint of the Taylor & Francis Group, an informa business

Library of Congress Cataloging-in-Publication Data
A catalog record has been requested for this book

ISBN: 978-1-138-63588-3 (hbk)
ISBN: 978-1-138-63590-6 (pbk)
ISBN: 978-1-315-20633-2 (ebk)

Typeset in Bembo
by Taylor & Francis Books

CONTENTS

1

REFLECTING ON REFLECTIVE PRACTICE

If you ask people if they are reflective in nature, most will answer affirmatively and many will agree that reflection is a good thing. Many are also able to quote Socrates: "The unexamined life is not worth living" and also most likely agree with him. This idea has also taken hold in many professions such as law, medicine, engineering, and education to name but a few. Therein lies a problem; because so many think they understand what it means to reflect, and what reflective practice is, the fact is that there are probably as many different definitions of reflection as there are people who purport to practice it, even though they rarely define it. The point is that when I say "reflection" there seems to be a common perception that we all mean the same thing; however, there still is not a consensus in all of the professions of what reflection really is or even what it entails. Although I go into much more detail about definitions of reflection and reflective practice in Chapter 1, it is safe to say that to be reflective generally means to be aware of what has happened, what is happening and possibly what will happen, although the level of awareness will differ from person to person.

Within the field of education reflection and reflective practice has also become popular with perhaps its main appeal simply, according to Loughran (2000) that it rings true for most teachers as something useful to follow. Indeed, as McLaughlin (1999: 9) has noted, "Who would want to champion the unreflective practitioner?" The general consensus is that teachers who are encouraged to engage in reflective practice can gain new insight of their practice and even become better teachers. I agree that teachers can gain a lot of insight related to their practice as a result of engaging in reflective practice, but we are still not sure if such reflection can or will actually improve practice or even if "improvement" is the desired end result. I will return to this latter point again in Chapter 8 after all the studies have been reviewed and are ready for appraisal that includes what the end desired result is or should be.

Reflective practice has also become popular in most TESOL teacher education and development programs recently. In fact, it was predictable that the popularity and enthusiasm exhibited with the concept of reflective practice in general education studies would eventually reach the field of teaching English to speakers of other languages (TESOL) as this crossover has occurred many times in the past with other concepts. However, this crossover was easier than most because of its simple appeal that teachers, including language teachers, should think about what they do and why they do it. Thus, many language teacher education programs warmly embraced the idea of encouraging TESOL teachers to reflect on their practice both as pre-service teachers as well as in-service teachers in development programs.

My first encounter with this complex yet intriguing concept happened when I too became curious about what I was doing in my language class and why in the late 1970s and led me to investigate the concept in more detail through the field of general education because TESOL was such a young field at that time and had not developed much of its own knowledge-base and thus relied on other fields such as education, psychology and linguistics. I discovered the concept of reflective practice on my own really and read about John Dewey's ideas of reflective practice for students and teachers and was impressed, and then Donald Schön's work in the early 1980s really set my developing interest along the path of reflection and indeed, led me to write my first book on the subject from this general educational perspective (see Farrell, 2004). I have since spent the intervening years encouraging TESOL teachers (and teacher educators) to engage in reflective practice and this book *Research on reflective practice in TESOL* is my latest attempt not only to continue encouraging language teachers and language teacher educators to reflect on their practice, but also to show how this concept has been researched in recent years within the field of TESOL. As you read the contents of this book, I think you will agree that the concept is truly a part of TESOL in its own right with the number of research articles devoted to the practices that encourage TESOL teachers to reflect. I review and appraise these articles but also I realize we still have a long way to go with TESOL as we need to be cognizant of whose traditions, approaches and methods we are mirroring when we as language teacher educators encourage TESOL teachers to reflect. Although you will read more about this in Chapter 8, when we cite Dewey or Schön's work or even my own work, we must realize that these are different in tradition and approach. Thus both teacher educators and teachers must define what they mean when they say they are engaging in reflective practice. One thing I can say for sure is that after reviewing these articles, I am more than confident that TESOL researchers, teacher educators, teachers and administrators can use this research that has occurred *within* TESOL as a basis for defining what reflective practice is. All I am doing is cautioning against hasty referencing to legitimize an approach without *full* understanding of that approach and its theoretical grounding. Thus I hope the contents of this book can help teacher educators when discussing what reflective practice in TESOL means and how it is done.

Reflective Practice in TESOL

I mentioned above that the concept of reflective practice has been warmly embraced within the field of TESOL since the early 1990s, and especially since Richards and Lockhart's (1994) excellent book on reflective practice which basically "translated" much of the research in general education studies and methods on reflection for the TESOL market. Since then the concept has been growing in popularity. However, we have not had a comprehensive review of what research has been carried out in TESOL related to the practices that encourage TESOL teachers to reflect in their own right and indeed, there is still no common agreement within TESOL (and general education studies) on what we really mean by "reflection" or "reflective practice" or what we mean when we say we encourage language teachers to reflect. What usually happens is that authors, speakers and teacher educators write, talk and encourage reflection but they do not really define what they mean about this complex topic that their probably have "translated" from general education research, nor have they attempted to trace what and who from the field of educational studies have influenced their understanding of the concept. In fact, few language teacher educators take the time in their courses to have their students discuss what they (teacher educators) mean when they say "reflection" or "reflective practice" or what their students think "reflection" or "reflective practice" is that they are asked to engage in. What invariably happens is that TESOL programs promote that their students are encouraged to engage in reflective practice as they want to develop reflective teachers and so they are asked to write "reflective" journals, engage in "reflective" discussions and so on, all with the wink and a nod that we all have a common understanding of what this "reflection" entails. They do not actually define what "reflection" is.

In an interesting recent article that criticizes this lack of attention to defining what we mean by reflective practice in TESOL, Mann and Walsh (2013: 292) maintain that such a lack of clarity can have negative consequences for teachers in training as well as experienced teachers as it can lead some to view reflective practice "as a management tool – used to measure and check teachers' performance, possibly to criticise and admonish." The danger here of course is that reflective practice has become ritualized – or just "gets done" (Mann & Walsh, 2013: 293) – and mechanical because we reduce this "reflection" to a set of prescriptive techniques and recipe-following checklists teachers much follow as they "reflect." Indeed, a persistent issue that has been often cited with reflective practice recently is that the many approaches in TESOL are too narrow because they view reflection solely as an intellectual exercise and neglect the emotional dimension of reflection (Akbari, 2007). I will address these perceived shortcomings in more detail in Chapter 8.

In addition to the criticisms related to definitional problems, background theoretical influences and the like, the reality is that, beyond anecdotal evidence, within the field of TESOL we do not know what actual research has been conducted and published in academic journals on the practices that encourage TESOL teachers to engage in reflective practice. As Mann and Walsh (2013: 292) have noted, although reflective practice "has achieved a status of orthodoxy" in the field of TESOL, this has happened, "without a corresponding data-led description of its value, processes and impact." Hence, I believe that it is both timely and important to provide an account of the body of research work which exists on the practices that encourage TESOL teachers to reflect, and also to examine and evaluate research that outlines the various approaches and theoretical grounding, contexts, topics of reflection and reflective tools used that encourage TESOL teachers to reflect on their practice. These are the basic aims of the book: *Research on reflective practice in TESOL*, as the title suggests. I agree with Akbari (2007: 205) when he noted: "It is good to reflect, but reflection itself also requires reflection."

Research on Reflective Practice in TESOL

Search and Selection of Studies

I confined studies to recent research reports in international journals of the last seven years (2009–2015) to ensure the sample represented current work within a strict time frame. I discovered a total of 138 studies related to the practices that encourage TESOL teachers to reflect. My search included many (but was not limited to) of the following domains (key words): (a) general terms: reflect, reflection, critical reflection, collaborative reflection reflective practice, reflective practitioner, reflective teaching, teacher development, teaching practice, L2 teacher reflection, teacher reflection, language teacher, second language teacher education, teacher education, teaching English as a foreign language, teaching English to speakers of other languages, TEFL, TESL, TESOL, English-language teaching, classroom practice, and combinations of all of these; (b) More specific terms related to practice (I can only provide a sample because of space restrictions): identity (teacher, professional), teacher development/support group, action research, analyzing cases, critical incidents, classroom communication/observation, critical friend, peer coach/mentor, peer observation, teacher belief/practice, teacher journals, reflective writing, self-monitoring/reflection, teacher metaphors, teacher narratives and combinations of all of these.

The resources and database I used were: ERIC, LLBA, MLA International Bibliography, Sociological Abstracts, Education Research Complete and other Internet collections on the Web as well as over 60 academic journals (all peer reviewed) which included (but are not limited to) some of the following: *Applied Linguistics, Applied Linguistics Review, Asia Pacific Journal of Education, Asia-Pacific Education Researcher, Asia-Pacific Journal of Teacher Education, Australian Journal of Teacher Education, Canadian Journal of Applied Linguistics, Canadian Modern Language Review, Classroom Discourse, Computers & Education, Educational Action Research, ELT Journal, English Teaching: Practice and Critique, European Journal of Teacher Education, Foreign Language Annals, Innovation in Language Learning and Teaching, Iranian Journal of Language Teaching Research, Journal of Education for Teaching: International Research and Pedagogy, Journal of Language Teaching & Research, Journal of Pan-Pacific Association of Applied Linguistics, Journal of Teacher Education, Language, Culture & Curriculum, Language Learning & Technology, Language Teaching, Language Teaching Research, Modern Language Journal, New Zealand Studies in Applied Linguistics, Professional Development in Education, Recall, Reflective Practice, RELC Journal, System, Teacher Development, Teachers & Teaching, Teaching and Teacher Education, TESL Canada Journal, TESOL Quarterly, TESOL Journal, Theory and Practice in Language Studies,* to name but a few.

Table 1.1 outlines how the results of the search (distributed in descending order from 2015 to 2009 inclusively) for studies related to the practices that encourage TESOL teachers to reflect.

Straight away we can see that there was a steady growth in these studies from 2009 with only six studies noted in the search but from 2011 it has risen and has been a consistent mid-20s number from 2011 onwards to a total of 138 studies over this seven-year period and this only in academic journals.

Review and Appraisal of Studies

In order to begin this review I had to come up with particular questions that I could follow as an initial guide for choosing articles on reflective practice related to TESOL teachers. The questions were devised after reading several articles on research in reflective practice from the field of general education and especially articles by Collin, Karsenti, and Komis (2013), Cornford (2002),

TABLE 1.1 Number of studies published each year

Year	Number of studies
2015	22
2014	23
2013	26
2012	20
2011	22
2010	19
2009	6

and Marcos, Sanchez, and Tillema (2011). Some of the main points extracted from the above articles that I considered important when deciding which articles were initially important enough to be included in the review were as follows:

- We still have a lack of theoretical clarity and consensus on the very concept of reflective practice.
- Sometimes it is difficult to actually observe reflective practice "in practice."
- We still have a lack of effort to evaluate the practical effectiveness of various approaches by empirical methods and through that the ideological positions that they represent.
- We still do not know if reflective teaching approaches result in improved practice.
- We need to distinguish between articles that disseminate evidence-based knowledge about reflection, rather than statements of opinion and belief.

Thus, the following questions then were used as an initial guide (but not set in stone) when choosing such studies:

- Does the study define reflective practice?
- Does the study observe reflective practice "in practice"?
- Does the study suitably operationalize reflective practice?
- Does the study ground itself in evidence, built on experiences, and/or empirical findings that can justify what is said to be done?
- Does the study distinguish between evidence-based knowledge about reflection, and statements of opinion and belief?
- Do we over-rely on case studies and non–quantitative methods and do we have any current moves towards empirical research employing both quantitative and qualitative approaches?
- Does the study give demonstration of significant long-term benefits?
- Does the empirical evidence establish that reflective teaching approaches have resulted in superior teaching or learning about teaching for both pre-service and in-service TESOL teachers?
- Does the study offer evidence-based or research validated information on what works in reflective practice?
- Does the study show specifically how teachers can attain grounded practices as well as evaluate the difficulties of implementing what is promoted about reflection?

Methodology

Although my own interest in the concept of reflective practice is long standing (e.g., Farrell, 1999a,b, 2001, 2004, 2006, 2008, 2012, 2013a,b,c,d, 2014a,b,

2015a,b, 2016, 2017), from the very start of this review, I was immediately faced with the formidable challenge of coming up with a methodology that would coherently present and analyze the vastness of the literature (138 studies) I encountered. So, as I began to undertake this somewhat daunting challenge of achieving my goal of providing an introduction to research on reflective practice in TESOL which is comprehensive, relevant, and accessible to researchers, teacher educators, administrators, and policy makers, I began to reflect deeply on my understanding of what it means to encourage teachers to engage in reflective practice, given that the concept is still "ill-defined, and … used rather loosely to embrace a wide range of concepts and strategies" (Hatton & Smith, 1995: 33). In addition, some scholars have maintained that one of the foremost methodological criticisms related to research on reflective practice is that because of the lack of theoretical grounding for the concept of reflective practice, the research conducted is too diverse to be compared (Collin, Karsenti, & Komis, 2013).

Therefore, I was looking for some way of comparing the vast amount of research articles devoted to reflective practice in TESOL and decided to use my own recently developed *framework for reflecting on practice* as a lens through which to compare the studies because the framework is both a "reflective" and a "reflexive" approach to reflective practice (for more on the framework see Farrell, 2015a). As Thompson and Pascal (2012: 320) have noted, the former incorporates the more "traditional notion of reflection as an analytical process" and the latter, reflexive approach emphasizes "the mirroring of practice, and thereby under-taking a self-analysis." I should note again that the framework is also a response to a recent widely cited criticism of the narrowness of many of the approaches used to encourage reflective practice (regardless of the field of study) that have often viewed reflection and reflective practice solely as a one-dimensional, intellectual exercise, while overlooking the inner life of teachers where reflection can not only lead to awareness of teaching practices but also self-awareness for a more holistic view of reflection and reflective practice (Akbari, 2007; Erlandson, 2006; Mann & Walsh, 2013; Thompson & Pascal, 2012).

A key factor behind the presentation of the research studies on the practices that encourage TESOL teachers to reflect through this descriptive *framework for reflecting on practice* is that it is grounded in the belief that teachers are whole per-sons and that teaching is multi-dimensional and as such includes the moral, ethical and spiritual aspects of what we do. As Akbari (2007: 201) has also (correctly) cautioned, within the field of TESOL when reflection becomes a solely intellec-tual exercise, reduced to a set of techniques, it leads to "a real loss of reflective spirit" and a "disregard for teacher personality." Thus reflective practice is grounded not only in the context but also in the person; the teacher can be separated from the act of teaching.

The framework I use to report on the studies in this review encompasses a holistic approach to reflective practice that focuses not only on the intellectual, cognitive and meta-cognitive aspects of our work, but also the spiritual, moral and emotional non-cognitive aspects of reflection that acknowledge the inner life of teachers; thus I define reflective practice in the introduction (although I tackle definitions of reflective practice again in Chapter 1) as: "a cognitive process accompanied by a set of attitudes in which teachers systematically collect data about their practice, and, while engaging in dialogue with others, use the data to make informed decisions about their practice both inside and outside the classroom" (Farrell, 2015a: 123). I fully admit that my definition is not conclusive as I continue to gain understanding of this fascinating concept.

I believe using this framework for methodological purposes and its perspective on reflective practice and teaching can provide an overall understanding on what research has been conducted on the practices that encourage TESOL teachers to reflect. We will be better able to not only examine the research but also see where it falls with such a comprehensive framework and by doing so we may gain more insight into directions for future research if particular areas of the framework are oversubscribed or undersubscribed. In addition, I believe that such a methodological approach to understanding the research on reflective practice in TESOL can provide further insights for teacher education, teachers, and teacher educators, administrators, and policy makers on the nature and processes of teacher reflections before, during and after practice so that reflection can be operationalized in more meaningful ways which are sensitive to the context and individual teacher. I also hope *Research on reflective practice in TESOL* will contribute to our understanding of this interesting but complex concept and the growing interest by language teachers themselves about what they do and why they do it and thus what it means to be a TESOL teacher so that they are stimulated to continue their reflections on practice.

Outline of the Book

Chapter 1 gives a general introduction to the book. The chapter starts with an introduction to reflective practice in the field of teaching English to speakers of other languages (TESOL). The discussion points to the need to reflect on reflective practice in TESOL because of its growing popularity. Then the chapter outlines how the studies were selected and the methodology used to present the vast number of studies that were chosen to represent the practices that encourage TESOL teachers to reflect. A key factor in the presentation of the book is that it presents a holistic picture of reflection through the lens of the framework for reflecting on practice.

In Chapter 2, I explain the concept of reflective practice in its historical context by outlining the origins of reflective practice in general education studies and how it has migrated to the field of TESOL. I then outline the various definitions of reflective practice in TESOL and what these mean for teachers and teacher educators. The contents of this chapter suggest that within TESOL we must be cautious about hasty referencing of a particular scholar's work on reflective practice without a full understanding or critical examination of its meaning. This suggests that not only should TESOL teachers take time to define what they mean by reflective practice but also language teacher educators and administrators.

Chapter 3 focuses on research conducted on the philosophy of practice and its various combinations with principles, theory, practice and beyond practice of TESOL teachers (pre-service and in-service) and most studies reported that as a result of engaging in such reflections, they could better understand their TESOL teacher identity: its origins, formation and development. The contents of the studies reviewed thus suggest that when TESOL teachers are encouraged to reflect on their philosophy combined with the other stages in the framework for reflecting on practice, they gain more self-knowledge and become more self-aware through such reflection that includes accounts of who we are and how and why we decided to become a teacher.

Chapter 4 outlines and discusses research conducted on the principles of practice and its various combinations with philosophy, theory, practice, and beyond practice of TESOL teachers (pre-service and in-service) and most studies reported that as a result of engaging in such reflections (mostly through metaphor analysis and reflective writing), they became more aware of their assumptions, values and beliefs about teaching and learning. The contents of the studies reviewed thus suggest that when TESOL teachers are encouraged to reflect on their principles combined with the other stages in the framework for reflecting on practice, they are better able to (re)evaluate their assumptions, beliefs and conceptions of teaching and learning and make modifications or complete changes to these if these were still appropriate.

Chapter 5 outlines and discusses research conducted on the theory of practice and its various combinations with philosophy, principles, practice, and beyond practice of TESOL teachers (pre-service and in-service) and most studies reported that as a result of engaging in such reflections (mostly through lesson planning analysis), pre-service TESOL teachers were able to build repertoires and knowledge of instruction while in-service TESOL teachers benefited most from accessing their theory though collective and collaborative lesson-planning conferences. The contents of the studies reviewed thus suggest that when TESOL teachers are encouraged to reflect on their theory combined with the other stages in the framework for reflecting on practice, they become more aware of their lesson planning details and the realization of the possibility of different types of instruction available as a result of collaborations with peers.

Chapter 6 outlines and discusses research conducted on practice and its various combinations with philosophy, principles, theory, and beyond practice of TESOL teachers (pre-service and in-service) and most studies reported that as a result of engaging in such reflections they became more aware of what they do in a lesson but that such awareness is best facilitated by receiving some kind of feedback during pre- and post-observation conferences in groups of some form (e.g., with or without video recordings of the lessons). The contents of the studies reviewed thus suggest that when TESOL teachers are encouraged to reflect on their practice combined with the other stages in the framework for reflecting on practice, they become more aware not only of their actual teaching behaviors, but also how this impacts and is impacted by their identity, beliefs, planning and the context they teach in.

Chapter 7 outlines and discusses research conducted beyond practice and its various combinations with philosophy, principles, theory, and practice of TESOL teachers (pre-service and in-service) and most studies reported that as a result of engaging in such reflections they were able to take a more critically reflective position towards their profession and as a result found the process transformative. The contents of the studies reviewed thus suggest that when TESOL teachers are encouraged to reflect beyond their practice combined with the other stages in the framework for reflecting on practice, they are not only able to reflect on their own assumptions, beliefs, and theories and how they could use this information to improve their practice, but also beyond practice and how these are all connected to wider school and social issues.

Chapter 8 examines the reflective instruments or tools that were used in the studies to help facilitate and encourage TESOL teachers to reflect on their practice. The results indicated that the main reflective tools used to encourage and facilitate reflection in the studies that were reviewed, discussion (including teacher discussion groups and post-observation conferences) was the most frequently used in this body of research, followed by journal writing and this closely followed by classroom observations (self, peer, etc. with or without video/audio), and then by lesser frequency action research, then narrative and lesson study. Reflective instruments such as cases, portfolio, team teaching, peer coaching, and critical friend/incident transcript reflections were used three or fewer times in the review studies.

Chapter 9 provides a general appraisal of the research results that were presented in the previous chapters through the lens of the framework for reflecting on practice. The chapter first outlines and discusses the participants, setting and methodology used in the studies and this is followed by the general appraisal of the research that was reviewed in the previous chapters. Overall, the research indicates that both pre-service and in-service TESOL teachers are interested in, and feel they benefit from, reflecting on various aspects of their practice. In addition, the positive impact reported in most of these studies on the increased level of awareness that is generated from such reflections seems to provide further opportunities and motivation for TESOL teachers to further explore and in some instances even challenge their current approaches to their practice, especially when they note any tensions between their philosophy, principles, theory and practice both inside and outside the language classroom.

Distinctive Features of the Book

The book is written in a clear and accessible style and assumes no previous background in language teacher education or reflection. Native speaker teachers and non-native speaker teachers alike will be able to interact with the contents of the book because of its accessible writing style and comprehensible vocabulary.

In each chapter after this introduction I have included sets of Reflective Questions where teachers/researchers/administrators can stop to reflect on particular questions related to the studies presented in that particular section. As this is a book that reports on studies related to reflective practice in TESOL, I think it important for readers to step back and reflect on what has been presented. I attempted to provide a wide range of questions to suit all types of readers, so please decide which ones are of most interest to your particular context.

Readership

Never before have we had any collection devoted to research on the practices that encourage TESOL teachers to reflect on their practice. So, this book is suitable for researchers interested in conducting research in reflective practice especially within the field of TESOL as well as graduate students doing theses (MA and PhD). It is also suitable for pre-service TESOL teachers in training, novice TESOL teachers, and very experienced TESOL teachers wishing to carry out studies in reflective practice in TESOL. This book is also suitable for program administrators and supervisors who are responsible for providing professional development opportunities for novice and experienced TESOL teachers and can use this review as a "library" of sorts to guide their understanding of reflective practice in TESOL.

I wish you all a pleasant reflective journey with the contents of this book and I hope by reading the research on the practices that encourage TESOL teachers to reflect you will be inspired to carry out your own research within your context and encourage other TESOL teachers to reflect on their practice.

2

DEFINITIONS

Introduction

As mentioned in Chapter 1, reflective practice is now a common term mentioned in the literature and advertisements related to most teacher education and development programs worldwide. In fact, it is nearly impossible to come across any teacher education program that does not purport to subscribe to reflective practice in some manner. This is true also in the field of teaching English to speakers of other languages (TESOL) and many language teacher education programs say that they promote and encourage reflective practice because they suggest it is beneficial for pre-service TESOL teachers as well as for in-service TESOL teachers. This is all promoted and encouraged with the idea that everyone knows and understands what it means to be a reflective teacher, not to mention how to go about this. However, many of these same programs do not define what reflection or reflective practice is, or at least how they define it and the tradition that is represented behind such a definition or what they mean by encouraging their participants to reflect.

What usually happens is that teacher candidates enter a program and take courses in which they are encouraged to "reflect" and this "reflection" is carried out for the most part, according to Mann and Walsh (2013), through the medium of writing (e.g., teachers are asked to write a journal refecting on various aspects/ issues they encounter in a course); all without much thought whether writing promotes reflection or not. Teacher candidates and/or in-service teachers may or may not be given guidelines about how to reflect and what to reflect on but they are rarely given definitions or full explanations of what reflection or reflective practice is. I suspect that many teacher educators themselves are not aware of the various different models of reflective practice that are in place and the varying different theoretical frameworks that have implications about how reflection should be practiced. More than likely what is really happening in many of these teacher education or development programs is the promotion (usually unwittingly, as I do not think that many teacher educators actually engage in evidence-based reflective practice themselves) and reaffirmation of their own teacher educator's beliefs about what (and how) the pre-service and in-service TESOL teachers *should* be reflecting on.

This is not to blame teacher educators or teachers for taking reflection at its face value of just "thinking about what you do" and getting on with it, because over the past 20 years reflection and reflective practice may have lost some of its true meaning and teacher educators may have reduced it to checklists to make it easier to comprehend not only from their perspective but also for their pre-service and in-service TESOL teachers. The issue really is that the renewed interest in reflective practice from its origin with the wonderful work of John Dewey in the 1930s and then Donald Schön's excellent re-examination not only of Dewey's work but also his own contributions have led to a huge development in approaches, models and frameworks that can be difficult to understand, especially as to their theoretical underpinning, and as a result we are left now with many different models that have different and unexamined conceptual and ideological positions. So it is no wonder that teacher educators and teachers have had a tendency to confine reflection and reflective practice to more narrow retrospective roles of what, why, now that approaches where the process of reflecting has become more ritualized and mechanical with teacher educators encouraging teachers to use recipe-following checklists as a means of promoting reflective practice.

This has all led to a stage of confusion within TESOL (and I suspect also in other professions as well) as to how TESOL teachers should be encouraged to engage in reflective practice. Carl Rodgers (2002: 843) has observed some important issues associated with a lack of a clear definition of reflection that is pertinent to this discussion thus far that teachers and teacher educators alike can consider when encouraging TESOL pre-service and in-service teachers to reflect:

- It is unclear how systematic reflection is different from other types of thought. Does mere participation in a study group, or keeping a journal, for example, qualify as reflection?
- If a teacher wants to think reflectively about or inquire into her practice, what does she do first? How does she know if she is getting better at it? To what should she aspire?
- How do we assess this skill of reflection as it is vaguely defined? Are personal ruminations enough or are there specific criteria for reflection?
- The lack of a common language means that talking about it is either impossible, or practitioners find themselves using terms that are common but hold different meanings or are different but have overlapping meanings (e.g., reflection, inquiry, critical thinking, metacognition).

- Without a clear sense of what we mean by reflection, it is difficult to research the effects of reflective teacher education and professional development (e.g., inquiry groups, reflective journals, or book clubs) on teachers' practice and students' learning.

I hope that the contents of this chapter and the review of the research of the practices that encourage TESOL teachers to reflect on their practice can give a bit more clarity to the points raised above by Rodgers (2002), in that readers will have more knowledge about actual approaches, practices, tools and contexts where reflection is encouraged worldwide. I will attempt not only to address these questions in this chapter but also throughout the book and return to them again in the final chapter.

Reflective Questions

- How would you define reflection and reflective practice?
- Do you think that reflective practice as a concept has lost some of its meaning?
- Do you think it has become everything to everybody and just a bandwagon?
- Examine each problem posed by Rodgers above and discuss each in turn.

This chapter outlines and discusses how the concept of reflective practice was defined (or not defined) and explained in the 138 published research studies on the practices that encourage TESOL teachers to reflect. In an attempt to address some of the shortcomings of the lack of clarity on its meaning, the chapter also examines what it means to reference particular approaches when attempting to legitimize their own particular method of reflection. The chapter concludes with a discussion on the importance of administrators, language teacher educators and teachers becoming more aware of their own definitions and understanding of what it means to reflect and encourage TESOL teachers to engage in reflective practice. This awareness should include a thorough understanding of whose tradition their definition and approach is mirroring and what this means so that everyone is clear about what reflection and reflective practice entails.

Defining Reflective Practice

As noted already, reflective practice has proliferated over the past few decades, especially since Donald Schön's work in the 1980s renewed interest in the concept mostly as a quest for the empowerment of teachers and out of the need to find some way to counteract a resurgence of teacher burnout in the teaching profession (Farrell, 2008). Indeed in many professions reflection has taken on the role of assessor and become one of the defining features of a practitioner's competence (i.e. are you a reflective practitioner?). For some individual practitioners it can be used (and abused) to rationalize some approach that in fact may be detrimental in some manner to others who "receive" the reflections. I believe within TESOL too, the ambiguity about what it means to reflect and the uncertainty over the definition of reflective practice can pose a serious problem for teacher education and development programs because different definitions and their associated different theoretical underpinnings will have different implications for its implementation. Thus it is important to consider what reflective practice means before teacher educators encourage TESOL teachers to practice it.

Of the 138 studies published in academic journals reviewed over the last seven years, it is interesting to note that only 52 of those studies defined (with citations) what their understanding of reflective practice is, 11 studies attempted to define or very loosely defined the concept, while a total of 75 studies (or over 50 percent of the total) did not give any definition of the concept. Although only 52 articles actually defined what they mean by reflection and/or reflective practice (I discuss this in more detail later in the section), all of the studies used terms interactively in the sense that they had the same meaning or understanding such as *reflection, reflective practice* and so on, some of which are outlined in more detail in Table 2.1.

As Table 2.1 indicates, many different terms were used (and many studies used multiple terms) but they all had the word "reflection" somewhere, but as I also noted, many of these studies (75) did not actually define the meaning of these terms, nor did they use any particular citation to show what theoretical framework they were working from or influenced by. So, as Rodgers (2002) suggested that there was a lack of clarity of what "reflection" looks like in general studies, this also seems to be the case within the field of TESOL where we think we have an understanding of terms without actually defining them. This is a serious issue for TESOL because without such clarity in what we mean by reflective practice, it makes the concept difficult to talk about in teacher education programs and courses as well as in in-service programs and courses. We need a common language and understanding about what these terms mean before we can encourage TESOL teachers to engage in reflective practice.

Many of the studies in the review use many of the different terms above without any explanation about what they mean or represent perhaps with the misconception that we have a common understanding of what they mean or should mean. This is of course problematic for the field of TESOL because as Ecclestone (1996: 153) has correctly pointed out, "Completely different models of knowledge and learning can underpin ideas about reflective practice."

As we can see from the details above there is still a lack of clarity in definitions of what reflection and reflective practice is in TESOL. Thus in order to gain a better understanding of what each study was trying to emphasize following the work of Akbari, Behzadpoor, and Dadvand (2010). I broke down the different terms used in all the studies into the different components and processes in reflection and reflective practice; they outline six different components of

TABLE 2.1 Terms used

Terms used	Number of studies
reflection	30
reflective practice	17
critical reflection	10
reflection-in-action	10
reflection-on-action	8
reflective practitioner	6
reflective teaching	6
reflective action	4
descriptive reflection	3
reflection-for-action	3
reflection-in-practice	3
reflective thinking	3
analytic reflection	2
dialogic reflection	2
reflection-on-practice	2
reflective inquiry	2
self-reflection	2
technical reflection	2
content reflection	1
contextualized reflection	1
evidence-based reflective practice	1
practical reflection	1
premise reflection	1
process reflection	1
reflecting on beliefs and practices	1
reflection-for-practice	1
reflective	1
reflective cycle	1
reflective decision making	1
reflective dialogue	1
reflective qualities	1
reflective skills	1
reflective teacher	1
reflectivity	1

reflective practice: *practical, cognitive, learner, metacognitive, critical,* and *moral.* Each component is explained as follows:

- *Practical* refers to the actual practice of reflection and the associated tools used when reflecting such as journal writing, lesson reports, surveys and questionnaires, audio and video recordings, observation, action research, teaching portfolios, group discussions, and analyzing critical incidents.
- *Cognitive* is concerned with the processes involved in reflection when engaged in professional development and includes such practices as action research projects, attending conferences and workshops, and reading the professional literature related to such development.
- *Learner* includes any instances the teacher reflects on the learner, learning and their responses including their emotional reactions.
- *Metacognitive* refers to teachers' reflections on their beliefs about teaching and learning including their affective make up as they define their practice.
- *Critical* deals with reflections on the socio-political aspects of practice such as race, gender and social class.
- *Moral* looks at justifications of practice from a morality perspective such as justice, empathy and values. I used these for coding and sorting purposes and I remained open to finding other components that would emerge from the analysis of the descriptions of reflection and related terms in the literature.

I then superimposed this component breakdown onto the terms of all 138 studies to see how the categories would fit in an attempt to evaluate the focus of these studies. Table 2.2 outlines these categories (with some overlap) regarding the 138 studies that were reviewed over a seven-year period (2009–2015).

TABLE 2.2 Components of reflective practice, 2009–2015

Component	Description	Number of studies
Practical	Actual practices of reflection and associated tools used	44
Cognitive	Processes involved in reflection and professional development	56
Metacognitive	Teachers' reflections of their own beliefs and personality, as well as the way they define their practice	45
Critical	Reflections on the socio-political aspects of pedagogy	11
Moral	Teachers reflecting on moral issues	3
Learner	Instances where teachers reflect on students; how they are learning, and how they respond and behave emotionally in the classroom	6

As Table 2.2 indicates the most common component in the 138 journal studies related to the practices that encourage TESOL teachers to reflect was cognitive (56), followed by metacognitive (45) and practical (44). These were the top three in terms of frequency, followed somewhat distantly by critical (11), learner (6), and moral (3). I now outline each in more detail and in order of frequency of most popular to least popular.

Cognitive

As can be observed in Table 2.2, the cognitive component of reflective practice was most in focus, with 56 studies included within this component when all were analyzed using the Akbari, Behzadpoor, and Dadvand (2010) framework. This focus of reflective practice, which includes teachers making a conscious effort to direct their own professional development by attending conferences and reading the literature on English language teaching and learning, has been the focus of much previous research (e.g., Farrell, 2004, 2015a; Richards & Farrell, 2005). In fact, many of the TESOL teacher studies, both pre-service and in-service, in this review encouraged such development by not only having reading components of various journal articles but also incorporated small scale action research projects as well.

One study, for example, outlined how teacher educators initiated a project aimed to encourage a critical stance towards the academic literature they were reading as well as a critical stance towards teaching theory used in teaching methods courses (Dooly & Sadler, 2013). These educators wanted to get their teacher learners to move from a "knowledge telling" to a "knowledge trans-forming" position as reflective practitioners. Dooly and Sadler (2013: 8) explained their approach to reflective practice as one in which "student-teachers are encouraged to critically examine their values, assumptions, theories and strategies that underlie their behavior and then take informed decisions in their teaching." In such a cognitive approach to reflective practice teacher educators encourage teachers to examine their philosophy, principles and theory as well as collect data about their own classrooms and use the data as a basis for self-evaluation and professional growth. As Lakshmi (2012: 193) has noted, such a self-directed approach to professional development involves teachers in an "ongoing process of examining their teaching and developing strategies for improvement." In addi-tion, such a cognitive approach to reflective practice means that teachers move beyond just reporting what happens in a class lesson on a particular day. As Sharil and Majid (2010: 262) have pointed out, teachers must be able to investigate the "whys" instead of just focusing on stating the "whats."

Reflective Questions

In order to reflect further on the *cognitive* component of reflective practice, for each question say whether the word *never, rarely, sometimes, often,* or *always* best describes your teaching practices (from Akbari, Behzadpoor, & Dadvand, 2010: 216). More importantly, try to give examples of each question from your practices:

a   I think of using/introducing new teaching techniques in my classes.
b   I read books/articles related to effective teaching to improve my classroom performance.
c   I participate in workshops/conferences related to teaching/learning issues.
d   I think of writing articles based on my classroom experiences.
e   I look at journal articles or search the Internet to see what the recent developments in my profession are.
f   I carry out small scale research activities in my classes to become better informed of learning/teaching processes.
g   I think of classroom events as potential research topics and think of finding a method for investigating them.

Metacognitive

The next popular component in terms of frequency of the studies analyzed was the metacognitive component with 45 studies focused on this component. This component, according to Akbari, Behzadpoor, and Dadvand (2010: 216), deals primarily with "teachers' knowledge of their personality, their definition of teaching and learning, and their view of their profession." The focus on a teacher's awareness of his or her personality is because, as Akbari (2007: 10) has pointed out, a teacher's "affective make up can influence their tendency to get involved in reflection and will affect their reaction to their own image resulting from reflection." One such study, for example, focused on pre-service teacher reflection as the teacher educators encouraged teachers to not only reflect on their beliefs, attitudes and knowledge of themselves and their practices but also at the same time to evaluate their students' learning outcomes (Hung & Yeh, 2013). In this way they hoped that pre-service teachers would become more aware of who they are as TESOL teachers.

Reflective Questions

In order to reflect further on the *metacognitive* component of reflective practice, for each question say whether the word *never, rarely, sometimes, often*, or *always* best describes your teaching practices (from Akbari, Behzadpoor, & Dadvand, 2010: 216). More importantly, try to give examples of each question from your practices:

a   As a teacher, I think about my teaching philosophy and the way it is affecting my teaching.
b   I think of the ways my biography or my background affects the way I define myself as a teacher.

c   I think of the meaning or significance of my job as a teacher.

d   I try to find out which aspects of my teaching provide me with a sense of satisfaction.

e   I think about my strengths and weaknesses as a teacher.

f   I think of the positive/negative role models I have had as a student and the way they have affected me in my practice.

g   I think of inconsistencies and contradictions that occur in my classroom practice.

Practical

The next popular component in terms of frequency of the studies analyzed was the practical component, with 44 studies focused on this component. This component according to Akbari, Behzadpoor, and Dadvand (2010: 215), deals with the "actual act of reflection by using different tools, such as keeping journals, talking to colleagues." However, it does not include partaking in an action research project as this is categorized under "cognitive" (above). The study by Lakshmi (2012) is an example of such an approach as it adopted various procedures and tools to help carry out reflections such as classroom observation, journal writing, and teacher support groups. When choosing which particular technique or combinations of techniques to use for reflection, Lakshmi (2012: 193) suggested that this was best left to the individual teacher to decide which "will serve his or her purpose."

Reflective Questions

In order to reflect further on the *practical* component of reflective practice, for each question say whether the word *never, rarely, sometimes, often,* or *always* best describes your teaching practices (from Akbari, Behzadpoor, & Dadvand, 2010: 216). More importantly, try to give examples of each question from your practices:

a   I write about my teaching experiences in a diary or a notebook.

b   I have a file where I keep my accounts of my teaching for reviewing purposes.

c   I talk about my classroom experiences with my colleagues and seek their advice/feedback.

d   After each lesson, I write about the accomplishments/failures of that lesson or I talk about the lesson to a colleague.

e   I discuss practical/theoretical issues with my colleagues.

f   I observe other teachers' classrooms to learn about their efficient practices.

g   I ask my peers to observe my teaching and comment on my teaching performance.

Critical

The next popular component in terms of frequency of the studies analyzed was the practical component, with 11 studies focused on this component. This component according to Akbari, Behzadpoor, and Dadvand (2010: 215), deals with the "socio-political dimension of teaching" and explores ways for achieving student empowerment. As Hatton and Smith (1995) suggest, when teachers take the social, political, and/or cultural factors into consideration when reflecting on their practice, they are engaged in critical reflection, but this is rare among pre-service teachers and this was also the case for this review, which was mostly conducted by in-service teachers. Chi (2013) for example, encouraged in-service TESOL teachers in Taiwan to engage in critical reflection when examining their beliefs and practices. As Chi (2013: 29) explained, this critical component of reflective practice is "an active, ongoing and social position with which the teacher-participants are engaged in exploring their classroom practice in a meaningful context." Farrell (2015b) also encouraged such a critical stance with in-service teachers as he encouraged TESOL teachers to reflect on the constraints mandated by the socio-political conditions in which the teachers work. Such a critical approach, according to Farrell (2015b), entails TESOL teachers transcending the behaviors of teaching and reflecting beyond just upgrading instructional techniques.

Reflective Questions

In order to reflect further on the *critical* component of reflective practice, for each question say whether the word *never, rarely, sometimes, often,* or *always* best describes your teaching practices (from Akbari, Behzadpoor, & Dadvand, 2010: 216). More importantly, try to give examples of each question from your practices:

a   I think about instances of social injustice in my own surroundings and try to discuss them in my classes.
b   I think of ways to enable my students to change their social lives in fighting poverty, discrimination, and gender bias.
c   In my teaching, I include less-discussed topics, such as old age, AIDS, discrimination against women and minorities, and poverty.
d   I think about the political aspects of my teaching and the way I may affect my students' political views.
e   I think of ways through which I can promote tolerance and democracy in my classes and in society in general.
f   I think about the ways gender, social class, and race influence my students' achievements.
g   I think of outside social events that can influence my teaching inside the class.

Learner

The next popular component in terms of frequency of the studies analyzed was the learner component, with only six studies focused on this component. This component, according to Akbari, Behzadpoor, and Dadvand (2010: 215), deals with "knowledge of learners and their affective/cognitive states," which includes reflecting on students' emotional responses in classes. Of the few studies that focused on the learner component of reflective practice, all noted the need to encourage teachers, especially pre-service teachers, to gauge their student reactions while they are teaching (reflection-in-action) and then adjust depending on these reactions (Akcan, 2010). Wyatt (2010) and Sharil and Majid (2010) also encouraged teachers to move from a technical focus on the self to more of a focus on learners and learning, again among pre-service teachers, by monitoring their students' responses during their classes.

Reflective Questions

In order to reflect further on the *learner* component of reflective practice, for each question say whether the word *never, rarely, sometimes, often,* or *always* best describes your teaching practices (from Akbari, Behzadpoor, & Dadvand, 2010: 216). More importantly, try to give examples of each question from your practices:

a   I think about my students' emotional responses to my instructions.
b   When a student is having an emotional problem or is neglected by his/her peers, I try to spend more time with him/her.
c   Before and after teaching, I think about aspects of my lessons my students liked/disliked.
d   I ask my students to write/talk about their perceptions of my classes and the things they liked/disliked about it.
e   I talk to my students to learn about their learning styles and preferences.
f   I talk to my students to learn about their family backgrounds, hobbies, interests and abilities.
g   I ask my students whether they like a teaching task or not.

Moral

The final component in terms of frequency of the studies analyzed was the moral component, with only three studies focused on this component. This component, according to Akbari, Behzadpoor, and Dadvand (2010: 215), deals with "issues of justice, empathy, and values" and includes three different approaches: deliberative (reflect on their moral purpose), relational (reflect on personal character) and critical. For example, in her review Yang (2009: 11) suggested that such a moral, critical stance to reflection by questioning personal underlying assumptions as well as challenging others to reflect on their assumptions is a way for teaching practices to be improved "and for the conditions in which schooling takes place to be more just." In addition, Sharil and Majid (2010: 263) noted that teachers who believe that they can have such an impact on children and school and schooling, "find new meanings and interpretations" and "care about others and contribute their time to social causes."

With all the different definitions, emphasis, and components connected to reflection and reflective practice, it is important for all TESOL teachers and teacher educators to define what it is, and what and who has influenced these definitions. As Fendler (2003: 20) has pointed out:

> Today's discourse of reflection incorporates an array of meanings: a demonstration of self-consciousness, a scientific approach to planning for the future, a tacit and intuitive understanding of practice, a discipline to become more professional, a way to tap into one's authentic inner voice, a means to become a more effective teacher, and a strategy to redress injustices in society.

This issue is addressed in more detail in the sections that follow, which discuss popular citations related to defining reflection and reflective practice as outlined in the studies under review.

Reflective Questions

In order to reflect further on the *moral* component of reflective practice, for each question say whether the word *never, rarely, sometimes, often,* or *always* best describes your teaching practices (from Akbari, Behzadpoor, & Dadvand, 2010: 216). More importantly, try to give examples of each question from your practices:

a   I think of my job as showing care and sympathy to others.
b   I regard myself as a role model for my students and as a result try to act as a moral example.
c   I believe in the concept of justice and try to show it in my classroom practice.
d   I talk about my moral standards and values to my students.
e   I establish a clear set of rules for my students to follow in terms of their classroom attendance and the way they will be evaluated at the end of the course.
f   I provide equal opportunities for all my students in the class regardless of their capabilities.
g   I have a clear set of general class rules and what constitutes acceptable behavior for my students to follow.

TABLE 2.3 Citations related to reflective practice

Outside TESOL	Number of studies
Dewey (1933)	19
Schön (1983)	22
TESOL	Number of studies
Farrell (2008)	10
Richards & Farrell (2005)	1

Citations of Reflective Practice

This next section addresses the different citations that were most popular from the 52 studies that defined reflective practice in order to discover which models of reflective practice underpinned these studies. Table 2.3 outlines the citations from the 52 studies that defined reflective practice and we can see that the main scholars outside TESOL that were cited are John Dewey (19 citations) and Donald Schön (22 citations) and within TESOL Thomas S. C. Farrell (10 citations plus 1 that includes work with Jack Richards).

Of course, again the immediate reaction is to note that more than half of the studies did not define reflective practice. Perhaps such scholars think that we all understand this concept because it is so popular, yet is it any wonder that teacher learners become confused when they are asked to "reflect" without being given a definition of what that concept is. In addition, of the studies that did define the concept, both John Dewey and Donald Schön were cited most frequently from outside TESOL and Farrell (this author) was most cited from within the TESOL literature.

The following are some representative example citations of John Dewey in many of the studies:

- Dewey (1933) refers to problem-solving thinking as reflection (Chen, 2012).
- Dewey (1933) made a distinction between "routine action" and "reflective action." Routine action is guided by factors such as tradition, habit and authority and institutional definitions and expectations. Reflective action involves willingness to engage in constant self-appraisal and development (Lakshmi, 2014).
- According to Dewey (1933) reflective thinking converts action that is merely appetitive, blind, and impulsive into intelligent action (Ryder, 2012).

The following are some representative example citations of Donald Schön in many of the studies:

- Schön introduced two labels to refer to different aspects of reflection in teaching: knowing-in-action and reflection-in-action. The former, a "repertoire of examples, images, understanding and actions" (Schön 1983: 138), which may be largely intuitive, is something that teachers draw on when confronted with an experience which is new or surprising, giving rise, in turn, to reflection-in-action. Schön described one final aspect to the reflective process, which he called reflection-on-action. This is the point in many teacher training programs when student teachers are invited to discuss and reflect upon a recent teaching experience (Ryder, 2012).

- According to Schön (1983, 1987) reflection can occur during classroom instruction or during reflection-in-action, and is seen as metacognitive action (Akcan, 2010).
- Schön suggested that not only is reflective practice presented as a tool for progression and improvement at a personal level, it has also been suggested that many professions now require formal evidence of reflection and development for continued eligibility for membership (Farr & Riordan, 2012).

Most of the above citations with accompanying "definitions" were placed as justifications for their use of reflective practice and some studies cited both scholars as justification. However, only one study attempted to compare and contrast the work of Dewey with the work of Schön. Yesilbursa (2011a) for example noted that while Dewey emphasized the scientific rationality of reflective thought, Schön viewed practice as an artistic and intuitive process. That said, nearly all the papers just made casual references to Dewey's and Schön's work without fitting it into any overall theoretical framework that signaled whose tradition the reflection was mirrored in for that particular study. In other words what we have now in TESOL research that encourages teacher reflection in teacher education and development programs is rather hasty referencing to both Dewey's and Schön's work without understanding what their approach really stands for. In the following section I will outline what it means to cite John Dewey and Donald Schön and later I will outline what it means to cite Farrell (this author) when it comes to encouraging TESOL teachers to engage in reflective practice.

Reflective Questions

- What is your understanding of the theory behind John Dewey's work related to reflective practice?
- What is your understanding of the theory behind Donald Schön's work related to reflective practice?
- What is your understanding of the theory behind Thomas S.C. Farrell's work related to reflective practice?
- Do you think all three work from the same theoretical framework?
- Why is it important to know whose tradition reflective practice is mirrored in before engaging in reflective practice?

John Dewey and Donald Schön

I now present both Dewey's and Schön's approaches to reflective practice in turn and the impact each has had on this important issue for teachers and teacher education. Because I am also cited within the field of TESOL I will then outline who and what have influenced my own recent framework/model for promoting reflection for TESOL professionals (Farrell, 2015a).

John Dewey

John Dewey is probably the most often cited scholar as the founding father of reflective practice and his book *How we think* (1933) is most referenced in the literature on reflective practice for teacher education and development. Dewey (1933) suggested that reflection is a special form of thinking and distinguished reflection from other forms of thinking, such as a stream of consciousness way of letting whatever comes into the mind at that time. So rather than allow thoughts to flow through the mind, Dewey (1933: 3) maintained that reflective thinking involves "turning a subject over in the mind and giving it serious and consecutive consideration." Such reflective thinking stems from as (Dewey, 1933: 12) pointed out, "a state of doubt, hesitation, perplexity, mental difficulty" related to an experienced situation.

Dewey (1933) viewed reflection as both a *process* (systematic) and a *product* (problem-solution). For Dewey the process begins with a teacher experiencing a situation which he or she finds problematic and considers some vague suggestions as possible resolutions of this situation. This reflective process involves the teacher engaging in reflective inquiry that starts with suggesting a possible solution (which he called "suggestion") followed by "intellectualization" where the difficulty or perplexity of the problem that has been felt (directly experienced) is intellectualized into a problem to be solved. Then one suggestion after another is used as a leading idea, or hypothesis; the initial suggestion can be used as a working hypothesis to initiate and guide observation and other operations in the collection of factual material. After that Dewey suggests that some kind of reasoning takes over and links present and past ideas and helps elaborate the supposition that reflective inquiry has reached, or the mental elaboration of the idea or supposition as an idea or supposition. Finally, the refined idea is reached, and the testing of this refined hypothesis takes place; the testing can be by overt action or in thought (imaginative action). For Dewey (1933: 116) the above steps (which teachers can experience in different sequences) represent the "indispensable traits of reflective thinking."

Thus for Dewey (1933: 9) reflective thinking is different from the usual routine thinking because as he suggests, reflection is guided by "active, persistent, and careful consideration of any belief or supposed form of knowledge in the light of the grounds that support it and the further conclusion to which it tends." The product of reflection is achieving the goal of alleviating the original doubt in reaching a solution. As Dewey (1933: 14–15) noted: "Demand for the solution of a perplexity is the steadying and guiding factor in the entire process of reflection … the nature of the problem fixes the end of thought, and the end controls the process of thinking." So by collecting data and a process of systematically thinking the problem out through hypothesis testing, trial and error testing of ideas and even revisiting different stages of his reflective inquiry process, we can reach an end solution or product of our reflection. As Dewey (1933: 104) pointed out: "Data (facts) and ideas (suggestions, possible solutions) thus form two indispensable and correlative factors of all reflective activity."

Dewey's (1933) principles of reflective practice are summed up nicely by Rodgers (2002: 845) as follows:

1. Reflection is a meaning-making process that moves a learner from one experience into the next with deeper understanding of its relationships and connections to other experiences and ideas. It is the thread that makes continuity of learning possible, and ensures the progress of the individual and, ultimately, society.
2. Reflection is a systematic, rigorous, disciplined way of thinking, with its roots in scientific inquiry.
3. Reflection needs to happen in community, in interaction with others.
4. Reflection requires attitudes that value the personal and intellectual growth of oneself and of others.

Of Dewey's four criteria for reflective practice summarized above, the necessity of having a reflective disposition or attitude is one of the most under referenced or encouraged in TESOL research. The attitudes a teacher brings to the reflective process are very important as Dewey noted, because positive attitudes can open the way for learning, while negative attitudes can block opportunities for learning. So it is also important for teachers to be aware of our attitudes and use them to promote learning for our students, thus our reflection as Dewey noted should be guided by open-mindedness, responsibility, and wholeheartedness. I will return to Dewey's affective dimension later in the chapter when I attach it to my own new framework.

Donald Schön

Much like Dewey, Donald Schön's seminal work, *The reflective practitioner* (1983) is very much cited by educators encouraging teachers to reflect (although Schön did not work with teachers in this book as he did in his later book, *Educating the reflective practitioner* (1987)).

Schön's model of reflection was developed after Dewey's model was criticized for its adherence to "technical rationality" and making meaning of experience in an overly systematic manner (or being too rational).

For Schön (1983: 31), technical rationality represents the "positivistic episte-mology of practice" where Schön (1983: 21) maintains "professional activity consists in instrumental problem solving made rigorous by the application of sci-entific theory and technique." Schön wondered what happens when practitioners are confronted with problems while they are doing something and must react spontaneously; Schön (1983: 49) was interested in studying these "artistic, intui-tive processes" that professionals (not necessarily teachers) develop though their careers because he recognized that such knowledge is difficult to explain because it is "tacit, implicit in our patterns of action and in our feel for the stuff with which we are dealing." Unlike Dewey, Schön (1983: 50) maintained that rational thought cannot account for such knowledge because the "know-how is *in* the action" and a feature of such "intelligent action." Such knowledge-in-action according to Schön is difficult to articulate by those in action because it is based on intuitive knowledge built up by skillful practitioners.

Schön's (1983: 54) now famous reflection-*in*-action or thinking about "doing something while doing it" occurs when something unexpected happens while doing and leads to a surprise. Such awareness occurs when as Schön (1983: 56) suggests, "intuitive performance leads to surprises, pleasing and promising or unwanted" and leads to explicit thinking about the action that is in progress or reflection during the action. Schön maintained that practitioners can become more aware of this tacit knowledge and learn from their knowledge-in-action. Schön (like Dewey) also recognized that practitioners can reflect when they are removed from that action, or reflection-on-action. Schön (1987: 28) explained reflection-in-action as involving a series of moments:

- Action that is routine, drawing on tacit knowledge occurs.
- An unexpected result of action causes a mismatch with previous knowledge.
- Reflection within the action takes place.
- Reflection-in-action questions the previous knowledge drawn on.
- Experimentation occurs.

So for Schön (1983: 276) reflection-in-action was at the center "intuitive knowing" that was the core of a practitioner's practice, in that problems that occur cannot be solved through the rigorous application of scientific approaches. For Schön technical rationalists were only concerned with rigor while he was more concerned with relevance that practitioners are confronted with in the midst of action. In his later book, *Educating the reflective practitioner*, Schön (1987: 22) sug-gested that the professional artistry that a practitioner displays revels in the "kinds of competence professionals sometimes display in unique and conflicted situations of practice." Thus they do not rely on espoused beliefs (what they say they believe) but on beliefs developed in and by action (or beliefs in use).

As discussed above, both Dewey and Schön have been cited in the research on the practices that encourage TESOL teachers to reflect. So because both scholars' approaches to reflective practice have become somewhat canonic in TESOL citations, it is important that they are fully understood so that teachers, educators and administrators are fully aware of the traditions they mirror. Up until now, both have basically remained unquestioned and uncontested in terms of what they actually represent.

The first aspect of understanding these two great scholars is that for both, reflection is triggered by some kind of experience and this experience results in the need to reflect in some manner. This results in the practitioner experiencing some kind of uncertainty that is usually a problem to be solved, either while it is being experienced (Schön) or after stepping back from it (Dewey). Dewey was more concerned with the process of reflection after the fact, and Schön how to facilitate that reflection while in the midst of action. For Dewey the problem would be ideally solved with reasoned and reflective thinking, but for Schön, although he does not disagree with Dewey (in fact Schön completed his PhD dissertation on Dewey's theory of inquiry), rather he builds on Dewey's ideas so for Schön ideally reflection is best accomplished in-action or while doing and this leads to a solution; but tacit knowledge must be revealed to the practitioner. Thus Schön builds on Dewey's ideas and taken together they emphasize reflection as reflection-*in*-action and reflection-*on*-action.

A Deweyan approach to reflection can be understood as an ends-based model where reflection is initiated by some problem in practice and this problem must be solved in a systematic and rational manner (reflection-*on*-action). By engaging in what Dewey (1933: 33) called reflective thinking, practitioners, he noted, can "act in deliberated and intentional fashion to attain future objects or to come into command of what is not distant and lacking." For Dewey (1933: 12) reflection must begin with some form of "shock or an interruption needing to be accounted for, identified, or placed." In addition, the ultimate aim of engaging in reflection is that it also must lead to a conclusive end; if not, the practitioner will need to repeat the five steps of his reflective inquiry until he or she solves the problem. There is no room for uncertainty in his approach to problem-solving and even though Dewey (1933: 114) realizes that the result of reflection may include a "failure to confirm a hypothesis," this failure will allow the practitioner to generate new solutions of "what further observations should be made."

A Schönian approach to reflection builds on the Deweyan idea of stepping back from a problem (or reflection-*on*-action) to include reflecting while doing (or reflection-*in*-action). Thus Schön (1983: 61) figured that the best way to facilitate reflection was not to abandon reflection-on-action that Dewey talked about, because he suggested that the practitioner can and should "think back on a project they have undertaken, a situation they have lived through" in order to "explore the understanding they have brought to their handling of the case." However, Schön (1983: 55) saw the need for practitioners to be able to reflect on action while in the middle of that action by "noticing situations, studying habits of thinking about patterns of action." For Schön this type of reflection would reveal what a practitioner is thinking about as he or she makes moment-to-moment decisions that are based on intuition for the most part. That said, I would suggest that Schön's reflection-in-action will always eventually lead to retrospective reflection-on-action moments as the practitioner considers the meaning in a distancing after the event. Thus we can say that similar to Dewey, Schön's approach to reflection proceeds along a causal chain that is also initiated by some problem or moment of uncertainty.

Reflection-*As*-Action

Both of the above approaches have influenced my own thinking of this complex concept of reflective practice over the years and my recent reflections of both approaches have led me to develop my own framework that builds on these approaches in different ways. I have attempted to include in my framework aspects of reflection that I think may be missing from these two approaches as follows.

When we look at both Dewey and Schön together we can see that for both, reflection is concerned with some kind of problem-solving, with Dewey's approach separating the person reflecting from the problem that he or she is reflecting on and for Schön, too, reflection-in-action has an intended end and eventually leads back to reflection-on-action. For Dewey and Schön reflection begins with a shock or some kind of uncertainty and for Dewey especially, there is no room for uncertainty and each problem must be solved. There is no means of reflection on situations that do not create uncertainty or doubt such as a pause to reflect on a teaching method that seems to work well. Because both approaches are fully focused on problem-solving, a practitioner's values are not included in any of the methods of reflection.

Both of these approaches are fine in themselves in that most if not all teachers are engaged each day in some kind of problem-solving. However, I note also that both approaches seem to separate the teacher as person who is doing the reflection from the problem that is reflected on. It seems that both scholars become somewhat fixated in solving the "problem" or "uncertainty" in a manner that separates the person and his or her emotions from the process. Bleakley (1999: 323) has maintained that such a gap in the reflective process can be removed if we think of the whole process in terms of "reflection-*as*-action" where reflection includes awareness of the personal self, the context as well as the problem to be solved. Thus reflection itself becomes a form of action and there is no separation between reflection and action (as in Schön's and Dewey's reflection-in-action and reflection-on-action).

Such a stance moves the concept towards a more holistic approach to reflective practice to include the emotional aspects of reflection that are missing in both Dewey's and Schön's approach. Although Dewey did comment on the position of emotion in reflection, he did not operationalize it in his model, a position I have since taken in my own recently developed framework that I explain in more detail below (and see Farrell, 2015a for more details). Indeed, I have attempted to build into my more holistic framework the spirit of what Dewey (1933: 278) wrote concerning the link between cognition and emotion in reflection:

> Human beings are not normally divided into two parts, the one emotional, the other coldly intellectual—the one matter of fact, the other imaginative. The split does, indeed, often get established, but that is always because of false methods of education. Natively and normally the person works as a whole. There is no integration of character and mind unless there is fusion of the intellectual and the emotional, of meaning and value, of fact and imaginative running beyond fact into the realm of desired possibilities.

The framework I use to report on the studies in this book encompasses a holistic approach to reflective practice outlined above in that it focuses not only on the intellectual, cognitive and metacognitive aspects of practice, but also the spiritual, moral and emotional non-cognitive aspects of reflection that acknowledges the inner life of teachers that are missing in both Dewey's and Schön's approaches. But rather than replace these wonderful approaches (after all I see myself standing on the shoulders of giants), I add to them and include the whole person as teacher as well as the issues that teachers want to reflect on.

The framework has five different stages/levels of reflection: *philosophy, principles, theory, practice,* and *beyond practice*. Throughout the reflective process, teachers are encouraged not only to describe but also examine and challenge embedded assumptions at each level, so that they can use the framework as a lens through which they can view their professional (and even personal) worlds, and what has shaped their professional lives as they become more aware of their *philosophy, principles, theories, practices* and how these impact issues inside and *beyond practice*.

Philosophy

Philosophy, the first stage/level of the framework, can be considered to be a window to the roots of a teacher's practice, because having a philosophy of practice means each observable behavior has a reason that guides it even if the teacher does not articulate this reason. This first stage of reflection within the framework examines the "teacher-as-person" and suggests that professional practice, both inside and outside the classroom, is invariably guided by a teacher's basic philosophy and that this philosophy has been developed since birth. Thus, in order to be able to reflect on our basic philosophy we need to obtain self-knowledge and we can access this by exploring, examining and reflecting on our background – from where we have evolved – such as our heritage, ethnicity, religion, socioeconomic background, family and personal values that have combined to influence who we are as language teachers. In addition, Dewey does not consider reflection as stream of consciousness thinking but this stage of my framework considers such a mode of reflection or contemplation a precursor to Dewey's reflective thinking. Such contemplation includes just being in the world as thinking human beings moment-to-moment doing our daily chores in and out of consciousness or being ourselves. At this stage teachers can also engage in what Dewey called reflective thinking, which I think should include teachers talking and/ or writing about their own lives and how they think their past experiences may have shaped the construction and development of their basic philosophy of practice.

Principles

Principles, the second stage/level of the *framework for reflecting on practice*, include reflections on teachers' assumptions, beliefs, and conceptions of teaching and learning. Assumptions generally refer to what we think is true but we do not have proof of as they have not been demonstrated yet; however, we accept them as true for the time being. Assumptions are thus sometimes difficult to articulate for a teacher. Beliefs, in contrast, are somewhat easier to state, and there is a general acceptance of a proposition; in other words, it is accepted to be true by the individual who holds it. Conceptions are more of an overall organizing framework for both assumptions and beliefs and they can mediate our response to situations involving both. All three are really part of a single system, and thus difficult to separate because they overlap a lot, and, although I treat them separately in the framework, I see them as three points along the same continuum of meaning related to our principles. Teachers' practices and their instructional decisions are often formulated and implemented (for the most part subconsciously) on the basis of their underlying assumptions, beliefs and conceptions because these are the driving force (along with philosophy reflected on at level/stage one) behind many of their classroom actions. One of the many means that teachers have at their disposal when accessing their principles (assumptions, beliefs and conceptions) is exploring and examining the various images, metaphors and maxims of teaching and learning.

Theory

Following on from reflecting on our *principles*, we are now ready to reflect on our *theory*, the third level/stage of the framework. *Theory* explores and examines the different choices a teacher makes about particular skills taught (or they think should be taught) or, in other words, how to put their theories into practice. Influenced by their reflections on their philosophy, and their principles, teachers can now actively begin to construct their theory of practice. Theory in this stage/ level means that teachers consider the type of lessons they want to deliver on a yearly, monthly or daily basis. All language teachers have theories, both "official" theories we learn in teacher education courses and "unofficial" theories we gain with teaching experience. However, not all teachers may be fully aware of these theories, and especially their "unofficial" theories that are sometimes called "theories-in-use." Reflections at this stage/level in the framework includes considering all aspects of a teacher's planning (e.g., forward, central and backward planning – see below) and the different activities and methods teachers choose (or may want to choose) as they attempt to put theory into practice. As they reflect on their approaches and methods at this level, teachers will also reflect on the specific teaching techniques they choose to use (or may want to choose) in their lessons and if these are (or should be) consistent with their approaches and methods they have chosen or will choose. In order to reflect on these, they will need to describe specific classroom techniques, activities and routines that they are using or intend to use when carrying out their lessons. Another means of accessing our theory is to explore and examine critical incidents (any unplanned or unanticipated event that occurs during a classroom lesson, and is clearly remembered) because they can be a guide to a teacher's theory building.

Practice

Up to now, the framework has emphasized reflecting on *philosophy, principles* and *theory*, or the "hidden" aspect of teaching. If we think of all of the whole teaching process as an iceberg, we cannot see the part of the iceberg that is beneath the surface of the water (the "hidden" aspect) that is much larger than the visible part on the top. All we can see is the top of the iceberg, or 10 percent of the whole iceberg, and in teaching this constitutes our *practice*, the fourth stage/level of reflection in the framework. Thus, we are now ready to reflect on the more visible behaviors of what we do as teachers, our *practice*, and what actually happens in the classroom. Reflecting on practice begins with an examination of our observable actions while we are teaching as well as our students' reactions (or non-reactions) during our lessons. Of course, such reflections are directly related to and influenced by our reflections of our *theory* at the previous level and our *principles* and *philosophy*. At this stage/level in the framework, teachers can reflect while they are teaching a lesson (reflection-*in*-action), after they teach a lesson (reflection-*on*-action) or before they teach a lesson (reflection-*for*-action). When teachers engage in reflection-*in*-action they attempt to consciously stand back while they are teaching as they monitor and adjust to various circumstances that are happening within the lesson. When teachers engage in reflection-*on*-action they are examining what happened in a lesson after the event has taken place and this is a more delayed type of reflection than the former. When teachers engage in reflection-*for*-action they are attempting to reflect before anything has taken place and anticipate what may happen and try to account for this before they conduct the lesson.

Beyond Practice

The final stage/level of the framework entails teachers reflecting *beyond practice*. This fifth stage/level of the framework takes on a sociocultural dimension to teaching and learning, which Johnson (2009: 2) points out is "not simply a matter of enculturation or even appropriation of existing sociocultural resources and practices, but the reconstruction and transformation of those resources and practices in ways that are responsive to both individual and local needs." This is sometimes called *critical reflection* and entails exploring and examining the moral, political and social issues that impact a teacher's practice both inside and outside the classroom.

This stage also includes the impact of the context (of which Schön's approach in particular ignored) in which the reflection takes place on the reflective process and thus moves the teacher *beyond practice* and links practice more closely to the broader socio-political as well as affective/moral issues that impact practice. Such a critical focus on reflections also includes teachers examining the moral aspect of practice and the moral values and judgments that impact practice. Again, this stage of reflection seems to be missing from both Dewey's and Schön's approaches. At this stage of reflection, we shift the focus of reflection from a somewhat decontextualized philosophy look at the individual towards how the overall five stages of reflection are interwoven and embedded to produce a total reflective result.

The framework stages briefly outlined above should not be seen as a separation of reflection into distinct categories that are separate from each other; rather each stage is just that, a stage, and for meaningful reflection to take place, teachers should combine the outcomes of their reflections at each stage to make a whole because each stage connects to the next and so on. However, teachers depending on their experience and interest may consider navigating the framework from different angles such as a theory-into-(beyond) practice approach starting with philosophy and moving through the different stages as outlined above, or they can take a (beyond) practice-into-theory application where they reverse the reflective process.

The framework is descriptive rather than prescriptive, and this distinguishes it from many other models that view reflective practice as a prescriptive rubric of skills that are to be checked off or even used to teach as modes of reflection. Thus the framework describes different aspects of reflection that are not linear in approach and can be distinguished and differentiated analytically, thus breaking away from many other approaches and models of reflective practice that assume a sequential, consecutive and linear mode of reflective thinking (e.g., Kolb, 1984; Korthagen, 2001, 2010; Rodgers, 2002).

In addition, I also believe that in order to encourage teachers to engage in reflective practice and/or in order to have a meaningful reflective experience if reflecting on one's teaching, it is necessary to cultivate a reflective disposition suggested earlier in the chapter. Reflective practice then requires not only cognitive discipline but also emotional, affective discipline that is embedded in such a reflective disposition. In other words, I agree with Dewey's emphasis on the importance of the affective side of reflective practice and of being open-minded, responsible and wholehearted when engaging in reflective practice.

- *Open-minded*: For Dewey (1933: 30), being open-minded, and thus not empty-minded, a teacher must be willing to look at various different perspectives of an issue and be willing to accept "the possibility of error even if the beliefs are dearest to us." In other words, we must be willing to admit that we could be wrong about our closest held beliefs about teaching and learning and if so, we need to make changes to view what we now hold to be true and thus the limitations of our initial perspectives.
- *Responsibility*: For Dewey (1933) this attitude of being responsible means that we are realistic about what we are doing. As Dewey (1933: 32) points out, to be responsible is to "consider the consequences of a projected step." In other words we must be willing to take responsibility for what we do and what we think and not to try to blame others. We must consider that what we do has an impact on who receives it and so our teaching impacts our students and the society we live in. Having a responsible attitude means developing sensitivity to, and awareness of, the real-life meanings of what we do.
- *Wholehearted*: Dewey (1933) suggested that being wholehearted, or single-minded, means that teachers have a genuine enthusiasm for the content they are teaching and in this case it is English to speakers of other languages. This also includes awareness of the learning of English and the impact of the teacher's teaching of English to his or her students. I agree with Dewey when he noted that curiosity and enthusiasm for teaching English to speakers of other languages is essential to good teaching; just consider some of the teachers you had in your schooling experience who showed little enthusiasm for the subject they were teaching and the impact that had on your learning. That said, I also agree with Rodgers (2002), who warns about the context that tends to beat this wholeheartedness out of the teacher because of too many students, inflexible curriculum, too many tests and no time to collaborate with other teachers, which can lead to a bitter feeling. That is why reflection should lead to action in that teachers should stand up against such emotionally draining working conditions so that we can provide optimum learning conditions for our students.

Reflective Questions

- What is your understanding of John Dewey's approach to reflective practice?
- Experience, according to Dewey, is not what happens to you, it is what *you* do with what happens to you. What is your understanding of this?
- What is your understanding of Donald Schön's approach to reflective practice?
- Schön suggests that reflection-*in*-action is at the center of "intuitive knowing." What is your understanding of this?
- What is your understanding of Thomas S. C. Farrell's approach to reflective practice?

- What is your approach to reflective practice?
- What is your understanding of reflection-*as*-action?
- Are you open-minded and, if so, how is this manifested in your practice?
- How can TESOL teachers be responsible for their actions and consider the impact of what they do in the classroom?
- Rodgers (2002) gives an example of an ESL teacher teaching refugees and her realization that their level of English was far below what she had first thought. At first she thought they were lazy and resistant, but after a careful analysis she realized this was not the case. She had wanted them to read articles on sexual harassment but recognized that they were ill-equipped rather than lazy or resistant, and that her (the teacher's) desires (i.e., that the students were more advanced but they did not have basic vocabulary or pronunciation) were distorting the meanings of her students' learning. How can she take more responsibility for her decisions from now on?
- Why is it important to be wholehearted about the content you are teaching and the impact of teaching on our students?
- Reflect on the impact of teachers in your schooling past who showed indifference to the subject matter they were teaching and the impact this had on your learning.
- In this chapter I pointed out that it is important for each teacher educator and teacher to define reflection, for fear of it being dismissed because nobody knows what it is or what to look for. Now that you have read the contents of this chapter, outline whose tradition your definition of reflective practice best mirrors so that you can legitimize your approach to researching reflective practice (the contents of the remainder of this book).

Conclusion

The contents of this chapter suggest that within TESOL we must be cautious about hasty referencing of a particular scholar's work on reflective practice without a full understanding or critical examination of its meaning. Indeed this is the true meaning and spirit of reflective practice. I also outline my own understanding of who (Dewey and Schön) has influenced my own approach to reflection and how this has developed as an example of my critical reflection on the concept. Ultimately, each teacher, teacher educator and administrator must define their own meaning of reflective practice and in whose tradition they want to mirror such reflections. Thus the chapter closely scrutinizes and critically examines the main scholars' reflective practice work used to legitimize their various approaches so that we can attempt to capture the complexities of their different views. In such a manner I hope that when teacher learners are encouraged to engage in reflective practice and particular scholars are cited when reflection is defined, we will know more about whose tradition this reflection is mirrored in.

3

PHILOSOPHY OF PRACTICE

Introduction

Teaching as an act seems simple: we have a teacher (usually one) and students (usually more than one) where the teacher attempts to "teach" something to the students that they did not know or realize before and so the teacher has now made them aware of this and so we have a "lesson." To many people who are not teachers it seems that a teacher's actions during such a lesson are the center of that lesson and as such these actions seem to get more scrutiny than anything else. In other words we see a "teacher" and we see "students" and the teacher seems to perform in terms of his or her particular actions and behaviors which are visible to students and those observing. Sometimes an observer has a checklist of behaviors that he or she marks during an observation such as "students are talking", "students are on/off task", and so on. For the most part, however, the teacher as a person is not taken into consideration by the observer, nor does the observer consider the identity of the teacher or his or her prior experiences either learning or teaching. Rather the teacher is observed and evaluated based on a checklist of preconceived notions of what good teaching is in terms of behaviors and these behaviors must be visible and of course desired behaviors of "good teaching." What is usually ignored is a view of the human who is teaching, or the teacher-as-person, who initiates these behaviors and actions and the cognitive but invisible processes that take place that drive such behaviors and actions.

A reflective practitioner is a human being first and hence a "person" or in professional mode a "teacher-as-person" where the human is at the center of the act of teaching. As mentioned in the previous chapter, the first stage of reflection within the framework for reflecting on practice, examines the "teacher-as-person" and suggests that professional practice, both inside and outside the classroom, is invariably guided by a teacher's basic philosophy and that this philosophy has been developed since birth. In other words, the person (as teacher) cannot be separated from the act of teaching or "who I am is how I teach." A teacher's philosophy comes from a deep understanding of the self and how we have evolved thus far as human beings and how aspects of our background – from where we have evolved – such as our heritage, ethnicity, religion, socioeconomic background, family and personal values have combined to influence who we are now as TESOL teachers. Thus for a teacher to truly understand the scholarship of his or her teaching, he or she must begin with a sense of self-understanding. This chapter outlines and describes the research related to TESOL pre-service and in-service teachers' philosophy and its various combinations with other aspects of the framework such as with principles, theory, and practice and beyond practice; but the dominant focus of reflection is related to the teacher's philosophy. The review is divided into studies related to pre-service TESOL teachers' reflections and this is followed by studies related to in-service TESOL teachers' reflections.

Pre-service Teachers' Reflections on Philosophy

Philosophy

When the focus of pre-service teachers' reflections was solely their philosophy of practice, all of the reviewed studies revealed that a main topic that arose was pre-service TESOL teachers' concerns with teacher identity. These studies explored pre-service TESOL teacher identity, especially its origin, formation and development. Many of these studies outlined how the pre-service TESOL teachers explored their identity and its development through their personal histories, either through narrative and/or online discussions. Chik and Breidbach (2011) for example, using an online written format to facilitate reflection in a German context, report how pre-service TESOL teachers explored their language learning histories as a means of examining their teacher identity formation and its subsequent development, and as a result stated that the teachers gained an increase in their self-knowledge as they became more aware of their various teacher role identities. As Chik and Breidbach (2011: 558) noted, the "writing experience [online] sensitized the writers to roles that language teachers played in the classroom" and how they were formed and developed. Chik and Breidbach (2011) concluded that as these pre-service TESOL teachers reflected on their teacher roles and identity development, this knowledge not only informed them about their philosophy and how this may impact their practice but also that this knowledge can be transformative. This realization led them to further examine how they could better negotiate the now articulated teacher identity roles as they move forward in their teaching careers. Such an in-depth reflection, although threatening at the time, led these pre-service teachers to mostly reaffirm "their decision to become teachers" (Chik & Breidbach, 2011: 557). It is conceivable to posit that these pre-service TESOL teachers discovered that the reflection process allowed them to prepare for their future careers in a realistic manner because they considered what they would face when they went out to teach, or their imagined identities.

Lim (2011), using a combination of autobiographical essays followed by a concept mapping reflective activity, also reported how pre-service TESOL teachers reflected on their own personal histories in relation to their professional identity origin, formation and development in a Korean context. Lim (2011) noted that at that time, Korean pre-service TESOL teachers had few chances to critically reflect on their own histories, assumptions and beliefs about language teaching because it is unusual to have such a focus in a Korean TESOL teacher education program. So, Lim (2011) examined how teachers organized and interpreted their personal histories, prior experiences, and beliefs in relation to their professional identity formation and development. In particular, Lim (2011) encouraged the pre-service TESOL teachers to explore their identity in terms of a teacher's ability, or of the desirable qualities of a "good" English teacher connected to professional expectations embraced by the English teaching profession in Korea. Lim (2011: 979) discovered that such reflection on identity in terms of perceived ability was closely connected to the pre-service TESOL teachers' insecurity about their English language proficiency. This study raises the idea of TESOL teachers' confidence and professional identity as teachers of English as a foreign language (EFL) because they are non-native English teachers (NNESTs). As Lim (2011: 979) concluded, teacher identity formation is an ongoing process of "identification and negotiation of self-images, prior experiences in learning and teaching, and the roles and credentials of teachers promoted by institutional and broader social practices." Thus, Lim (2011: 979) suggests that because pre-service non-native speaker TESOL teacher identity, defined in terms of teaching ability, is closely linked to the teachers' acknowledged need to improve English proficiency, there is a strong need for TESOL teachers education programs in Korea to "expand English proficiency training courses as a core component of its curriculum." This result highlights the close correlation between a NNESTs identity and English proficiency level and as such, language teacher education programs may need to consider the needs of learner teachers rather than the needs of the faculty.

Similar to Lim's (2011) study noting the importance of context (South Korea) for language teacher education programs related to the needs of teacher learners, so too Trent (2010a) noted the importance of context (in this case Hong Kong) in constructing and shaping TESOL teachers' professional identity. Trent (2010a) observed that in the context of Hong Kong the particular group of TESOL pre-service English teachers tended to construct a rigid dichotomy between the professional identity positions of the "traditional" and the "modern" teacher and had more positive evaluations of the "modern" teacher identity but more negative evaluations of the "traditional" teacher identity. Thus Trent (2010a: 912) maintained that it is important to increase "trainee teacher's awareness of the multidimensional social universe in which teacher identities are constructed" because it is "an important step in overcoming such dualism." He pointed out that although this approach of getting the pre-service TESOL teachers to focus on how professional identity was constructed seemed to be successful, in that they were willing to be flexible in their thinking as a result of such reflections, nevertheless the context (Hong Kong with its reforms at that time) still weighed heavily on how the teachers constructed identity. As Trent (2010a: 912) reported: "The flexibility shown by these participants as they constructed their professional identities also needs to be situated within the context of the recent reforms to education within Hong Kong."

The influence of context on identity construction and development was further illustrated in a case study by Kong (2014) that explored the lived experiences and identity construction of one Vietnamese pre-service TESOL teacher while studying in Australia and how the teacher changed some aspects of her professional identity as she adapted to that context. According to Kong (2014: 90), the teacher (Thinh) arrived in Australia with a "strong professional background and a high self-esteem of herself as a proficient user of English in Vietnam but when she was in Australia, she was challenged in various ways, particularly outside class." Some of these challenges included the tension between upkeep of her English language proficiency when she spent time using Vietnamese with her Vietnamese friends as she attempted to achieve some balance with her new life in Australia and how to maintain (and indeed sometimes retain) her original Vietnamese language and culture. As a result of her intense reflection on who she was and who she wanted to be as a TESOL teacher in terms of her professional identity, she began to realize that she wanted to maintain aspects of her "old" identity that she brought with her from Vietnam because she found herself constantly thinking of home. The teacher realized that she was changing while living in Australia but recognized that when she returned to Vietnam, she would also face issues related to her identity. As Kong (2014: 89) observed, "She was aware of the challenges that she would face when she returned to Vietnam and reflected on ways to incorporate her own ideas within those constraints." Thus for this teacher (Thinh), teacher identity development involves some shifting back and forth depending on context and includes some continuity of the "old" identity and some change to incorporate developing or "new" identity. This will be especially important for those pre-service teachers of English who move to a context and/or country different from their place of origin to study and/or work as a TESOL teacher. Such knowledge of the idea of shifting identities for pre-service TESOL teachers who move back and forth between country of origin and the context of the language teacher education program will again be important for language teacher education programs to consider. As Kong (2014: 91) points out, teacher education programs should "provide reflective activities to help pre-service TESOL teachers understand and cope with the shifting of identity that will inevitably occur."

So far, the studies reviewed have had philosophy as their main concentration of reflection for pre-service TESOL teachers. In terms of combinations of pre-service

English teachers' reflections, philosophy was a main focus but it was also connected with other aspects of reflections, such as philosophy and practice, philosophy and beyond practice, and the combination of philosophy, principles, theory, practice and beyond practice for pre-service TESOL teachers.

Philosophy and Practice

Combining philosophy with reflections on practice, Kanno and Stuart (2011) examined a case study of the processes in which two novice TESOL teachers transition towards identifying themselves as second language teachers and how their emerging identities helped shape their classroom practices. Kanno and Stuart (2011: 249) noted that it takes time for pre-service TESOL teachers to develop their teacher identities and it is only when these novice teachers experienced a process of prolonged "learning-in-practice," that they "came to view themselves as teachers." It seems that as a result of this prolonged "learning-in-practice" the teachers noticed that their foreign language teacher identity formation brought with it greater confidence and authority. As a result, Kanno and Stuart (2011) maintain that TESOL teacher learning is not so much the acquisition of the knowledge of language teaching methodology and skills as it is the development of a teacher identity. In an interesting finding Kanno and Stuart (2011) also argue that the acquisition of knowledge is part of this identity development, but not the other way around. Indeed, they conclude that the novice TESOL teachers' evolving identities are probably the reason for the changes in their classroom practices. As Kanno and Stuart (2011: 249–250) explain, "changes in novice L2 teachers' classroom practice cannot be explained solely in terms of the changes in their knowledge; again, one needs to refer to their evolving teacher identities to fully understand why certain changes occur in their practice." However, in another interesting finding they observed that as novice teachers' identity became more solidified, they became more distant from their students; as Kanno and Stuart (2011: 249) report, in exchange for a "more established identity as a teacher, they grew more disengaged from their students."

Farr and Riordan (2015) also combined reflections of philosophy with practice as they encouraged pre-service TESOL teachers to reflect on their identity construction with the use of electronic communications. Farr and Riordan (2015: 18) report that as the teachers reflected on their identities through different types of reflective engagements, their reflections "appear to move to the more critical domain." It is interesting that for this combination of philosophy and practice, Farr and Riordan (2015: 15) reported that although they were encouraged to reflect on their practice as well as others' practices, they did "not reflect much on teaching but reflected merely on a personal level." They also discovered that the pre-service TESOL teachers developed another online identity and voice as well as observed others' online identities. As a result they point out the importance of discourse in identity construction and especially for the projection of identities because they say it allows people to shape, reshape and make sense of their teaching identities.

Philosophy and Beyond Practice

Barkhuizen (2010) used a combination of a reflection focus on philosophy and beyond practice, or stage 1 and stage 5 of the framework, as he encouraged a pre-service TESOL teacher to construct a series of personal reflective narratives to investigate teacher identity as it emerged in small stories-in-interaction. The main questions asked were "Who am I?" and "Who do I imagine myself to be in the future?" By examining the pre-service TESOL teacher's emerging identity as an English language teacher as she imagined her future working life within an imagined community of teachers and English language learners, Barkhuizen (2010) reported that she was then able to (re)evaluate and rethink ideas about teaching and her imagined roles within those communities. As Barkhuizen (2010: 296) noted, the teacher was able to "re-story her experiences of becoming a language teacher; and with each re-storying continue repositioning and re-imagining her own teacher identity." Such reflections helped this pre-service TESOL teacher to begin her transformation from a peripheral member of the community of teachers of English teachers (and learners) into a more legitimate future participant of that community.

Philosophy, Principles, Theory, Practice and Beyond Practice

In one study on pre-service TESOL teachers' reflections on philosophy combined with all the other stages of the framework, principles, theory, practice and beyond practice, Wach (2015) using e-mail correspondence in a Polish-Romanian setting encouraged pre-service TESOL teachers to link their self-knowledge with their beliefs (principles), theories, practices and system of education (beyond practice) so that they could become more aware of the impact of their overall training on their future careers. As a result, Wach (2015: 41) observed that such an activity "stimulated reflective conversations" and although for some pre-service teachers their reflections were not very deep, others "made attempts at deeper, more critical reflections by linking previous experiences to their present situation, and by making references to what their partner wrote and evaluating it critically." In such a manner, Wach (2015) noted that the pre-service TESOL teachers could consider their training and their forming identities as language teachers as well as reflecting on their future teaching career after graduation.

Reflective Questions

- TESOL teachers have many roles (inside and outside the classroom) to play that form part of their overall identity as teachers. Name the various roles teachers play inside and outside TESOL classrooms.

- What are desirable qualities or abilities of a "good" TESOL teacher?
- Kumaravadivelu (2012: 55–56) has pointed out that teachers' personal dispositions define whether they move towards becoming "passive technicians" and "conduits transmitting a body of knowledge" or "transformative intellectuals" and "change agents." What is your understanding of this statement with regard to a TESOL teacher's role identity?
- How is English language proficiency level linked to a pre-service TESOL teacher's identity?
- What is the place of English language proficiency improvement in a language teacher education program?
- How is a pre-service teacher's identity formation and construction linked to context?
- Why and how would a TESOL pre-service teacher shift back and forth to include some continuity and some changes in their identity development depending on context?
- Do you agree that teacher learning is not so much the acquisition of the knowledge of language teaching as it is the development of a teacher identity and that the acquisition of knowledge is part of this identity development, but not the other way around?
- Why do you think that in one study the researchers noted that as the pre-service teachers' identity became more solidified, they also became more distant and disengaged from their students?
- What is your answer to the questions: "Who am I?" and "Who do I imagine myself to be in the future as a pre-service teacher in an imagined community of teachers, teaching institutions and English learners"?
- Why would reflections on identity lead to pre-service teachers (re)considering the idea of taking up a teaching career after their graduation from the teacher education program?

In-service Teachers' Reflections on Philosophy

When in-service TESOL teachers were encouraged to reflect on philosophy, either solely or in combination with other aspects of their practice, similar to the studies reviewed above for pre-service TESOL teachers, issues were related to teacher identity and especially the idea of the possibility of a gap developing between teacher identity expectations versus reality, as was noted in the research reviewed.

Philosophy

When in-service TESOL teachers were encouraged to reflect solely on philosophy, Liu and Xu (2011), using a process they call "restorying" (see also Barkhuizen (2010) above for similar methodology), outlined how one novice teacher became aware of an identity gap between what the teacher felt she was expected to become (i.e., "designated teacher identity") and how she realistically identified herself (i.e., "actual teacher identity"). Similar to the Kong (2014) study, Liu and Xu (2011: 596) also discuss the idea of shifting identities but this time for in-service teachers as they discovered that the teacher shifted her identity (especially where there was competing identities at play) to adapt to different situations and based on "many rounds of reinterpretation of the self and the situation." They noted that in this relational process, a gap or some kind of disparity was always present between the teacher's designed identity (identity that is dictated by the dominant discourse of the community and a novice teacher feels "bound" to follow) and her actual identity (identity that is not bound and novice teacher is free to develop her or his own persona). To close this gap, Liu and Xu (2011: 594) noted, the teacher engaged in a process of making and remaking her identity by using different "positioning strategies based on the situational meanings that she derived from the context." The teacher then, as Liu and Xu (2011: 595) observed, created a process of "interplay between the self and the situation" in a "process of making and remaking of identity, with the aim of closing the gap between the designated and the actual identities." Being encouraged to reflect and thus becoming more aware of the possibility of shifting identities helped the teacher close the gap between her "designated" and "actual" identities. As Liu and Xu (2011: 596) observed, "identity is not static and fixed but negotiated and shifting" and that the very noticing of this shifting of her identity "has indeed helped shape her professional life."

Philosophy and Beyond Practice

Two studies examined reflections on in-service teachers' combination of philosophy and beyond practice (Farrell, 2014a; Mitton-Kükner & Akyüz, 2012). Farrell (2014a) looked at the reflections of three experiences ESL teachers from the same college as they participated in weekly group discussions and engaged in classroom observations and journal writing. The three teachers mentioned that they had reached a stage in their teaching careers where they felt they had plateaued professionally and as such wanted to critically reflect on their practice as a group with the aid of a facilitator. Farrell (2014a) reported that the main topics the teachers talked about were the university administration, their colleagues and the learners. These discussions started mostly with negative comments about the administrations but then moved to a more positive stance towards their colleagues and learners; as Farrell (2014a: 516) remarked: the "discussions follow a trajectory from the initial group discussions negative focus on their frustrations with the administration almost exclusively to more positive discussions about their colleagues and learners."

Farrell (2014a) discovered that these discussions helped the teachers break free of isolation and overcome feelings of plateauing as they were able to vent while at the same time systematically reflect on their roles and duties not only with the administration but also their colleagues and learners. Farrell (2014a) noted that one of the teachers was perhaps facing a teacher identity crisis before engaging in the reflective process but after the intense period of reflection she seemed to have renegotiated her identity thus moving her perceived "designated identity" to her "desired identity," similar to the Liu and Xu (2011) study reported above. In this case it was the regular group discussions that helped the teacher through the process of reinventing her professional identity and as Farrell (2014a: 515) reported, the teacher herself noted "in these discussions we validated each other's experiences, gave support, sympathy, encouragement, held up similar experiences for comparison, and compared our different teaching styles." In such a manner, each of the experienced TESOL teachers in the group conveyed that they were able to reinvent their teacher identities in a manner that suited their personal interpretation of their practice. As a result these experienced TESOL teachers were able to regain their enthusiasm for their work both inside and outside the classroom.

Similar to the Farrell (2014a) study reported above, Mitton-Kükner and Akyüz (2012) explored how two English university TESOL teachers in Turkey from different cultural backgrounds also met for weekly discussions in order to reflect on their practice. Specifically, Mitton-Kükner and Akyüz (2012: 432) focused "upon the meaning of two storied moments to consider how our collaborative inquiry into these instances contributed to our professional development." As a result of reflecting in such a manner, they reported that the teachers developed a new awareness of what was unfolding in their professional lives both inside and outside the classroom. Mitton-Kükner and Akyüz (2012: 438) remarked, "A significant aspect that emerged from our collaboration was newfound awareness of the social complexities shaping multiple places in our university context." Such a collaboration they noted, allowed both to unveil their storied experiences so that they could learn from each other about adapting practices and cultivating new awareness of their surroundings. For example, as they examined the metaphors embedded in their stories, they noted how inexperienced and uncertain they felt about their teacher identities because the university they were members of was in fact a competitive and ultimately lonely environment to work in. But because they had engaged in a process of reflection that allowed them to obtain a macro awareness of their particular context, they took on a transformative role as they (re)negotiated and developed a new professional identity to suit their present context. As Mitton-Kükner and Akyüz (2012: 435) observed, "Inquiring in this way enabled us to see possibilities in what had unfolded in a class and staff room, that is, new ways to understand these particular events in relation to who we were." Mitton-Kükner and Akyüz (2012: 439) concluded that by a process of "discussing their experiences they were able to focus on issues that were critically important and personally significant" to each of the teachers. Again and similar to Farrell (2014a) above, by being encouraged to engage in reflection, these TESOL teachers were able to move from feelings of isolation and uncertainty in terms of who they are as teachers to a more transformative and positive position of noticing the potential for professional learning as they move forward in their careers as TESOL professionals.

Philosophy, Theory, Practice and Beyond Practice

Several studies examined reflections on in-service TESOL teachers' philosophy, with combinations of theory, practice and beyond practice. Ahmadi, Samad, and Noordin (2013) for example, used small group discussions over a period of time to facilitate a group of in-service TESOL teachers' reflections on their philosophy, practice and beyond practice and reported that such discussions had a significant impact on their professional identity development as they became more professional members of the teaching community in Iran. Ahmadi, Samad, and Noordin (2013) observed an identity shift (see also Kong, 2014) during the course of the group discussions as the teachers obtained a new understanding and reconsideration and renegotiation of their professional teacher identities. Ahmadi, Samad, and Noordin (2013: 1765) observed that over time the teachers began to identify themselves as more legitimate members of their English as a foreign language (EFL) discourse community. Ahmadi, Samad, and Noordin (2013: 1766) further remarked that as the teachers experienced the professional identity transition and shift, they saw themselves as transformative individuals who could be more contributing to their local EFL community and "by voicing their professional self in the professional small group discussions, they could create a space for their active participation in their EFL discourse community." However, it is interesting to note that this group of teachers saw no necessity to engage in discussions or practices beyond their local TESOL community. One reason Ahmadi, Samad, and Noordin (2013: 1786) stated this was the influence of context; they continue, "a lack of writing support centers and writing tutors discouraged the in-service teachers from participating in the practices of the international TESOL discourse community through writing for publication." Ahmadi, Samad, and Noordin (2013: 1765) concluded that "a teacher's identity is a continuous process of being informed, formed, and reformed which develops over time mostly through having interactions with other members of their discourse community and also through reflection over teaching practices."

Similar to Ahmadi, Samad, and Noordin's (2013) study above, Farrell (2011b) examined the reflections on the specific role identities of experienced TESOL teachers through regular talk in a teacher reflection group in Canada and especially about who they are and how they have been shaped over time. Among the cluster of teacher roles the teachers identified, three were prominent in their careers: teacher as manager, "acculturator" and professional. Teacher as manager was categorized as a role where the teacher is the person attempting to manage what happens in the classroom. Among the more frequently mentioned sub-identities within the teacher as manager cluster were teacher as vendor ("selling" the language and the program) and teacher as entertainer. In particular the teacher as vendor role revealed that they were not satisfied with this identity as it was imposed by the administration but nevertheless as Farrell (2011b: 59) noted, they still choose to adopt the practices necessary to "keep the customers happy" in order to meet externally determined student retention goals. In contrast to this role the teachers took on the teacher role identity of teacher as "acculturator" where the teacher is seen as one who engages in activities outside the classroom that help students become accustomed to the local culture even though this was not technically in their job description. The most frequently occurring sub-identities in this cluster were of teacher as "socializer,' and teacher as social worker. Teacher as professional was also identified where the teacher is seen as one who is dedicated to her work, and takes it very seriously. There were further sub-identities within teacher as professional such as teacher as collaborator, and teacher as learner. The results of this study highlight the reality of the tensions between workplace expectations and their impact on practice both inside and outside the classroom that can cause tension, or as Pennington and Richards (2016: 6) have called it, "identity stress," when teachers feel pressure to conform to either a prescribed curriculum, and/or exam as well as retaining students. In many ways, and as Pennington and Richards (2016) have observed in other contexts, it seems that these experienced TESOL teachers had to compromise their approach (and as a result compromise their identity?) to satisfy both the institutional requirements as well as their own values as TESOL professionals.

In another study under this combination of philosophy, theory, practice and beyond practice, Chao (2015) examined the narrative reflections of in-service TESOL teachers' interactions with digital technologies in Taiwan and how they made changes to their teacher identity during and after an in-service course. As Chao (2015: 113) reported, because the teachers were encouraged to critically reflect on their use of technology and connections between digital learning, teaching and the context in which they teach, they experienced some "unexpected thoughts, classroom practices, and a change of teacher identity" that left a lasting impact on their classroom practices. Indeed, as Chao (2015: 113) observed, "the teachers were able to discuss how their teaching practices and teacher identities had been impacted on multiple levels of complexity." Chao (2015: 113) also reported that their reflections were not limited to computer assisted language learning (CALL) issues but these teachers were also motivated "to examine their teaching even when technology is not involved." In such a manner, it seems that the reflective process expanded beyond its initial focus to encompass all aspects of their professional practice both inside and outside the classroom.

Philosophy, Principles, Theory, Practice and Beyond Practice

The final combination of philosophy included all the categories together with principles, theory, practice, and beyond practice and included two studies in the review (Johnson & Golombek, 2011; Shelley, Murphy, & White, 2013). Johnson and Golombek (2011) explored the reflections of two TESOL teachers, one who kept a private reflective journal for an entire 15-week semester and another who was simultaneously enrolled in a distance-learning program to earn his Master's degree in teaching ESL. Johnson and Golombek (2011: 497) observed that for one teacher (Jenn) narrative reflection through verbalization allowed her to externalize her thoughts because such verbalizations allowed her "to regulate her thinking, and as a form of systematic examination that pushed her to describe, define, and explore her own learning as a teacher and the consequences of her interactions with her students in this classroom." The issue for the teacher was becoming clear through narrative verbalization that she was becoming more cognizant of her "desire to share power with her students" (Johnson & Golombek, 2011: 497). For the other teacher (Michael) in the case study, such narrative reflections also allowed him to externalize as he began to move from the "abstract to the concrete" but differently from the other teacher (Jenn), he (Michael) was able to make some behavioral changes in his practice. This was mainly because as Johnson and Golombek (2011) report, he became more aware of both his fears about, and the consequences of, his teaching behaviors. As Johnson and Golombek (2011: 504) observed, "Unlike Jenn, however, we see evidence of Michael gaining internal control over his teaching behaviors, changing both himself and his material activity, and resolving the emotional dissonance that initially drove his inquiry." Johnson and Golombek (2011: 504) point out that engaging in reflective practice allowed this teacher to "critically examine his own teaching behaviors, recognize the reasons behind those behaviors, and change both his thinking and his activity in ways that support all students' opportunities for learning." Thus, as a result of their engagement in systematic reflections and narrative verbalization of their professional development, one teacher reported a change in behaviors while the other reported gaining awareness of practice and articulated a desire to plan for future changes in practices.

In another study in the combination, Shelley, Murphy, and White (2013) also examined the reflections of two in-service TESOL teachers' identity development during their careers in order to consider the impact of the identity challenges and changes they had experienced, how they responded to those challenges and changes, and what had been most influential in that process. They used the construct of narrative frames (where teachers complete sentences) to help the teachers reflect. Similar to the emotional dissonance of reflection discovered in the Johnson and Golombek (2011) study above, Shelley, Murphy, and White (2013: 572) also reported that emotional dimensions of reflecting on identity were significant for the teachers and as a result, there was an "ongoing sense of contingency, that their current practices were emerging or provisional, that nothing was resolved or complete." As a result Shelley, Murphy, and White (2013: 572) concluded that when engaged in critical reflection, it is important for teachers to process and regulate emotion "in ways that are productive and facilitating." Such a realization that teacher identity is not only connected to rational choice but also emotions has also been noted in previous research on teaching and teacher identity (e.g., Benesch, 2012).

Reflective Questions

- Do you agree that a TESOL teacher's identity is a continuous process of being informed, formed, and reformed which develops over time, mostly through having interactions with other members of their discourse community and also through reflection over teaching practices?
- What is your understanding of a gap between what a TESOL was expected to become (i.e., "designated teacher identity") and how a TESOL identified herself (i.e., "actual teacher identity")?
- What is your understanding of the notion of shifting identities in a TESOL teacher's career?
- How can teachers in mid-career (re)evaluate their identities, especially when they feel they are plateauing and isolated?
- Why would context be an important consideration for a group of TESOL teachers' decision to limit their reflections on their identity development to their local TESOL community and not beyond to the international TESOL discourse community through writing for publication?
- Why would TESOL teachers still choose to adopt the negative practices to keep the customers happy in their role as "teacher as vendor" in order to meet externally determined student retention goals?
- Why are the emotional dimensions (e.g., emotional dissonance) of critically reflecting on identity significant for TESOL teachers?
- What is your understanding of identity stress that the TESOL teachers were experiencing as a result of their having to conform to institutional requirements?
- Do you think that TESOL teachers may need to compromise their teacher identity in order to satisfy institutional requirements if they clash with their own values as TESOL teachers? Explain your answer.
- Kumaravadivelu (2012: 58) has argued that "A crucial factor that will determine whether teachers succeed in forging a desired teaching Self is their ability and willingness to exercise their agency and to formulate strategies of power and resistance." What is your understanding of this statement for you as a TESOL teacher?

Conclusion

Most of the studies, both pre-service and in-service, outlined in this chapter were related in some manner to the issue of TESOL teacher identity when teachers were encouraged to reflect on their philosophy alone or in combination with other stages of the framework for reflecting on practice such as principles, theory, practice, and beyond practice. Most of these studies examined teachers' reflections on the origins, formation and development of teacher identity in the pre-service year as well as the in-service years. Some studies also noted the interesting notion of shifting identities for both pre-service and in-service teachers. So when teachers were encouraged to reflect on their philosophy through exploration of their personal histories, such reflection allowed the teachers to note how these teacher identities not only informed their practices, but also how they are open to critical reflection and change depending on the context. As most of the studies reviewed involved some kind of discursive reflections on teacher identity, they seem to agree with Haugh's (2008) premise that identities are not independent of discourse, but are realized via discursive practices. The contents of the studies reviewed thus suggest that when TESOL teachers are encouraged to reflect on their philosophy they gain self-knowledge and become more self-aware through such reflection that includes accounts of who we are and how and why we decided to become a teacher. Such reflecting on philosophy can be seen as the bedrock of a TESOL teacher's professional identity. The next chapter reviews studies related to the practices that encourage TESOL teachers to reflect on their principles of practice.

4

PRINCIPLES OF PRACTICE

Introduction

In the previous chapter I outlined and discussed a review of the studies related to when TESOL teachers are encouraged to reflect, where philosophy was the main focus of reflection and its various combinations with principles, theory, practice and beyond practice. In this chapter I proceed to review research related to the next stage of the framework, namely a teacher's principles, and review studies where the main focus is TESOL teachers reflecting on their principles and its various combinations with philosophy, theory, practice and beyond practice.

When TESOL teachers are encouraged to reflect on their principles, the second stage/level of the framework for reflecting on practice, they explore their assumptions, beliefs, and conceptions of teaching and learning in detail. Although assumptions, beliefs and conceptions all reflect a teacher's principles when it comes to teaching and learning there are some subtle differences between the three and as such can be placed along the same continuum. Assumptions can be at one end and seen as pre-beliefs because they have not really been demonstrated yet but they are in our heads as thoughts about our practice and thus difficult to articulate. Beliefs can be in the middle as they are more solidified and so we can articulate them more readily. Conceptions can be placed on the other side of this continuum because they can be seen as a type of overall organizer of both assumptions and beliefs and thus act as a mediator of our responses to situations involving both assumptions and beliefs. That said, I consider all three difficult to separate as they are intertwined and interconnected in many ways thus on the same continuum (for more on this see Farrell, 2015a). From a reflective practice perspective all three are of immense importance for a TESOL teacher because a teacher's behavioral actions we see in a classroom are often formulated and implemented (for the most part subconsciously) on the basis of that TESOL teacher's underlying assumptions, beliefs and conceptions of teaching and learning. So this chapter reviews such research related to pre-service and in-service TESOL teachers' principles and its various combinations with philosophy, theory, and practice and beyond practice. The review is divided into studies related to pre-service TESOL teachers' reflections and this is followed by studies related to in-service TESOL teachers' reflections.

Pre-service Teachers' Reflections on Principles

Principles

When the focus of pre-service TESOL teachers' reflections was exclusively on their principles of practice, all of the reviewed studies reported that as a result of engaging in reflection, the teachers reported a heightened awareness of their previously tacitly held assumptions, values, and beliefs about teaching and learning (e.g., Abednia, Hovassapian, Teimournezhad, & Ghanbari, 2013; Lin, Shein & Yang, 2012; Nagamine, 2012; Polat, 2010).

Abednia, Hovassapian, Teimournezhad, and Ghanbari (2013) for example, used reflective journals to encourage pre-service TESOL teachers in Iran to foster awareness of their beliefs about teaching and learning English as a foreign language and especially how their TESOL teacher education program course-content related or not to their real-life classroom teaching experiences. As a result of such reflections, Abednia, Hovassapian, Teimournezhad, and Ghanbari (2013: 507) observed that the pre-service TESOL teachers were able to "construct their own understanding of issues covered in the class in light of their personal experiences of teaching" as they became "more aware of their implicit beliefs" about English language teaching in their particular context. Articulation of their implicit beliefs according to Abednia, Hovassapian, Teimournezhad, and Ghanbari (2013), allowed the teachers to gain heightened awareness of their assumptions and beliefs and this awareness allowed them to evaluate and in some cases re-evaluate those beliefs in terms of their appropriateness. The pre-service TESOL teachers reported that they were then better able to identify their teaching strengths and areas needed for improvement and gain the overall freedom to be able to continually modify their existing beliefs whenever appropriate.

Lin, Shein and Yang (2012) also observed similar perceptions of freedom when they examined pre-service TESOL teachers' explorations of their beliefs of teaching and learning (mainly through metaphor analysis) in Taiwan. They reported that many of the pre-service TESOL teachers stated that they felt liberated because of their growing awareness of their own beliefs of language teaching and learning. Lin, Shein and Yang (2012: 193) conveyed that the most frequently represented conceptions of teaching based on the metaphor analysis were teachers "in the supporting and guiding roles of leader, nurturer, tool provider, and artist and in the prescribing and controlling roles of change agent, doctor and mechanic," while they noted that learners were represented by a wide range of metaphors from very active (for example, musicians, actors) to very inactive (for example, cars, and patients). Lin, Shein and Yang (2012) noted that they had no observational evidence to verify any concrete connections between their beliefs and classroom practices, but because they used metaphors "as translators of experience," they maintain that these pre-service TESOL teachers' conceptions of teaching is deeply rooted in their past experiences. Lin, Shein and Yang (2012) posit that as a result of their reflections, the pre-service TESOL teachers were better able to gain more control of their previous tacitly held beliefs and conceptions related to teaching and learning English as a foreign language. As Lin, Shein and Yang (2012: 196) remarked, the pre-service TESOL teachers were able to "liberate their thinking by distancing themselves, to a certain extent, from their everyday experiences" when reflecting on their beliefs and thus solidify their views of teaching and learning.

Nagamine (2012) also encouraged pre-service TESOL teachers in Japan to reflect on their principles again by using metaphor analysis to help the teachers verbalize their underlying beliefs about teaching and learning. Nagamine's (2012) study is important because he reported that some pre-service TESOL teachers tended to struggle to externalize their underlying beliefs because they had difficulty articulating them. Nevertheless, Nagamine (2012: 161) reported that overall such an exercise of articulating and analyzing metaphors increased the pre-service TESOL teachers' levels of reflectivity and led to the pre-service teachers reevaluating the appropriateness of their beliefs and even add some alternative metaphors as they "modified the reasoning behind [current] metaphors."

In another related study Polat (2010) encouraged pre-service TESOL teachers in Turkey to not only articulate and reflect on their beliefs but also to see if this new level of awareness would lead to any re-evaluation of their appropriateness. Polat (2010) asked the teachers to focus specifically on the issue of materials development, and especially the pre-service TESOL teachers' beliefs about the effectiveness of various aspects of authentic, commercial, and teacher-made materials. In such a manner Polat (2010) encouraged the pre-service TESOL teachers to move beyond articulation of their beliefs and reflect on their meaning regarding materials development and what they believed about the effectiveness of teacher-made materials compared to more commercially developed materials. As a result, Polat (2010) noted that the pre-service TESOL teachers were able to make specific adjustments to their beliefs about materials development. As Polat (2010: 203) remarked, "the participants altered some of their beliefs about the effectiveness of teacher-made materials compared to commercial and authentic materials." We can see that from the above studies that focused on encouraging pre-service TESOL teachers to reflect solely on their principles, many report that the teachers gained heightened awareness of their beliefs about teaching and learning as well as the capacity to transform these beliefs after more critical reflection.

Principles, Theory and Practice

Principles were also combined with other stages of the framework for reflections such as theory and practice and most of these studies reported on the transformative nature and value of reflective practice on both the pre-service TESOL teachers' beliefs, planning and classroom practices. Mak (2011) for example, encouraged pre-service TESOL teachers in Hong Kong to reflect on their beliefs, theories and classroom practices during their practicum experience, and especially to explore how their beliefs and theory interacted (or not) with their actual teaching decisions. Mak (2011: 63) discovered that for one teacher such discussions raised awareness about "her hidden desires to spell out everything she had prepared and to maintain control" over her teaching and that this may not be promoting student learning. As a result of such reflections, especially through post-observation discussions with her teaching adviser, Mak (2011: 63) noted that the teacher was able to "make some adaptions" to her beliefs as they related to her practices.

In China, Yuan and Lee (2014) also explored pre-service TESOL teachers' beliefs and planning before their teaching practicum and how they can also be transformed after reflection. They reported that the pre-service TESOL teachers changed their beliefs during and after the teaching practicum. When writing their reflections in their journals, Yuan and Lee (2014) remarked that the teachers shared their inner thoughts and beliefs about their tensions they felt between divergence or congruence of beliefs and practices and that as a result they could transform their beliefs as they attempted different approaches to their teaching practice. As Yuan and Lee (2014: 10) observed, "their beliefs were examined and transformed as they began to experiment with different approaches to teaching." In a similar type of study in Thailand, Day (2013) reported that the pre-service TESOL teachers, when reflecting on their beliefs, theory, and practice, not only responded positively and adapted beliefs, but also were able to make some changes to their teaching behaviors. In addition, the pre-service teachers continued with such peer observations after the practicum to help them continue reflective practice.

Using an action research approach to encouraging reflections on the connections between principles, theory and practice for pre-service TESOL teachers in Hong Kong, Trent (2010b) reported that pre-service teachers were able to contest their previously held assumptions and beliefs about teaching and learning English as a second language. As Trent (2010b: 158) observed, the action research project helped the pre-service TESOL teachers "contest their images of teachers and teaching" and "their alignment with some aspects of contemporary educational discourse." Trent (2010b: 165) pointed out that through such an action research project approach to reflective practice, pre-service TESOL teachers can experience a shift in previously held rigid beliefs with the resulting "opening of possibilities for new meanings of teaching and learning to emerge."

When the use of video reflections was added (to the other modes mentioned above) as prompts in post-observation discussions for reflection on beliefs, planning and practices, several studies reported that this helped the pre-service TESOL teachers make clearer connections between principles, theory and classroom practices which can lead to the teachers attempting to make changes to their practice. Tinker Sachs and Ho (2011: 274), for example, noted that the use of video in post-observation discussions helped their pre-service TESOL teachers in Hong Kong to "apply their theories and reflect on the soundness of their own beliefs and practices in clear and explicit ways."

Also using videos to help facilitate reflection in the US, Payant (2014) observed that pre-service TESOL teachers were able to reflect more productively on their linguistic abilities (their English language skills especially) and on their developing teaching identities (especially their non-native speaker teacher identity) as they attempted to make theory-practice connections. According to Payant (2014) the use of videos stimulated these teachers to examine not only how their beliefs and planning are connected to their practices but also motivated them to try out new teaching practices as they tracked their own professional development.

Similarly, in Brazil Kaneko-Marques (2015: 75) observed that during post-observation collaborative discussions with the use of video as prompts, the pre-service TESOL teachers were able to better establish "connections with theoretical course content, previous learning and teaching experiences, and their personal knowledge when analyzing their pedagogical actions in videotaped lessons." As a result of these reflections, Kaneko-Marques (2015: 75) noted that the pre-service TESOL teachers were better able to reconstruct their pedagogical practice to "favor their students' language learning process" and this contributed to "their professional development as educators" within their teaching context. Indeed, Kaneko-Marques (2015: 76) reported that video reflections helped the pre-service TESOL teachers become "more reflective and self-evaluative" because they were able to better identify problems and search for their own solutions. It was this final act of searching for their own answers that Kaneko-Marques (2015: 76) observed, allowed the pre-service TESOL teachers to examine and critically reflect on their beliefs and "their previous language-learning and teaching experiences and by theoretical and practical knowledge concerning language teaching and learning" so that they could better comprehend the language-teaching process in real school settings in Brazil.

Chick (2015) also looked at how exploratory talk during post-teaching practice discussions can be beneficial to pre-service TESOL teachers in the UK. They noted that such an approach may help promote long term reflective practice and how inquiry-based talk raises awareness of the complexity involved in developing pedagogic expertise. According to Chick (2015), talk in reflective group discussions can provide space for pre-service TESOL teachers to articulate their understandings of the teaching process and raise awareness of the complexity of teaching. As Chick (2015: 302) observed, such exploratory talk appears "to help the learner teachers notice aspects of practice and possibly reformulate their thinking about pedagogical issues." Such a process of reflection, according to

Chick (2015: 302), allowed the pre-service TESOL teachers to uncover their implicit beliefs regarding classroom actions, and thus led them to "probe their emerging understandings or encourage exploration of the teaching and learning process." This reflection also helped the pre-service TESOL teachers to "draw on and consider the theoretical aspects of their pre-service education and thus aid the reframing of their emergent understandings of language teaching" (Chick, 2015: 304). As such, Chick (2015: 306) proposes that TESOL teacher educators should encourage pre-service TESOL teachers to reflect at an early stage in their development to "raise awareness of the TESOL subject area knowledge base. This includes linguistic, theoretical, methodological, and procedural elements."

Some of the reviewed studies also used some form of online forums, chats and/ or blogs along with other reflective modes and instruments to encourage pre-service TESOL teachers to reflect on their principles, theory and practice. Fleming, Bangou, and Fellus (2011) for example, used online blogs (along with other reflective modes and instruments) in Canada to encourage pre-service TESOL teachers to reflect on their beliefs and reported it was a transformative experience for the teachers because they were able to change their pedagogical beliefs and opinions about teaching and learning a second language. As Fleming, Bangou, and Fellus (2011: 49) observed, the teachers not only developed "their opinions about second-language education" but also were able to "transform their pedagogical beliefs and theories about second-language education." In particular, as a result of reflecting on their prior beliefs, they noted that the pre-service TESOL teachers were critical of grammatically based lessons because of their own past experiences and suggested that more functional approaches be adopted. Indeed, similar to Chick's (2015) conclusions above, Fleming, Bangou, and Fellus (2011: 54) conclude that TESOL teacher education programs should emphasize early that reflective practice is "anchored in the social nature of learning" and that this is "central to ESL teacher training."

Yang (2009) also used blogs to encourage reflection in post-observation discussions about principle, theories and practice. Such discussions according to Yang (2009) created a community of practice (CoP) which stimulated more critical reflection and discovered that, although there was high and interactive participation among the pre-service teachers in the CoP, overall their reflections tended to be more descriptive than critical in nature, mainly because they feared offending others and damaging friendships. Yang (2009) again noted the importance of facilitator (in this case the teacher educator) intervention before the pre-service teachers were able to feel comfortable about expressing any negative thoughts or reflections. Yang (2009) reported that such a CoP blog provided a platform for the pre-service teachers to reflect on their learning and teaching and allowed for more critical or challenging discussions with peers than would have been the case in face-to-face discussions.

Taking the notions of online blog reflections and CoPs further, Yu-Chih Sun (2010) used reflective cyber communities (or 'blogospheres') in Taiwan to encourage pre-service TESOL teachers to reflect on their beliefs and theories of teaching and learning. These blogospheres, according to Yu-Chih Sun (2010: 380), "allowed students to participate actively as knowledgeable, reflective, creative, and critical members in cyber communities." The results were reported as being largely positive, as the pre-service TESOL teachers began to reshape their beliefs and theories while blogging in the blogospheres.

Farr and Riordan (2012) and Riordan and Murray (2010), both working in Ireland, likewise noted the different degrees of reflection when using online chats and discussion forums to encourage reflection in post-observation discussions. In their study, Farr and Riordan (2012) noted that discussion forums were found to have comparatively low interactivity and little reflection while online chats were highly interactive and more reflective. As a result of their confirmation that different modes of online reflection result in varying degrees of reflection, Farr and Riordan (2012: 144) recommend that pre-service teachers be given a "variety of tasks and modes" because they suggest this "will result in a more rounded reflective experience." Riordan and Murray (2010: 181) also made use of interactive online discussion forums and chats to encourage their pre-service teachers in Ireland to reflect on their principles and theories of teaching and learning and noted that these online modes of reflection also "facilitate[d] reflection and support[ed] problem solving." That said, they argue that chats may be better for pre-service teachers than forums because chats allow for more time to reflect. I will return to this issue of different instruments/modes of reflection again in Chapter 8.

Reflective Questions

- What is your understanding of the differences between a teacher's assumptions, values, beliefs and conceptions of teaching and learning?
- How does articulating teachers' underlying assumptions, values, beliefs and conceptions of teaching and learning aid a teacher's reflections on their appropriateness for a particular context?
- Why do you think pre-service teachers may feel liberated as they became more aware of their own beliefs of language teaching and learning?
- Why and how would pre-service teachers' conceptions of teaching be deeply rooted in their past experiences?
- Why would some pre-service teachers struggle to externalize their underlying beliefs or have difficulty articulating their beliefs about teaching and learning?
- One study discovered that for one pre-service teacher, reflections on beliefs, planning and practice raised awareness about her hidden desires to spell out everything she had prepared and to maintain control over her teaching and that this may not be promoting student learning. What are your hidden desires about your practice?

- How can the use of videos as prompts help stimulate teachers to examine their beliefs, planning and practices and motivate them to try out new teaching practices after such reflections?
- Why do you think that discussion forums were found to have comparatively low interactivity and little reflection while online chats were highly interactive and more reflective for examining beliefs, planning and practice?

In-service Teachers' Reflections on Principles

When in-service TESOL teachers were encouraged to reflect on principles, either solely or in combination with other aspects of their practice, similar to the studies reviewed above for pre-service TESOL teachers, in-service TESOL teachers have also reported heightened awareness of their beliefs and as a result of this knowledge, some were able to re-evaluation their appropriateness in light of their greater awareness.

Principles

When in-service TESOL teachers were encouraged to reflect exclusively on principles, Borg (2011a), for example, through a process of reflection that included coursework, teaching practice and feedback, and reflective writing, examined the impact of in-service education on TESOL teachers' beliefs in a Delta program module in the UK which had as one of its main aims to develop candidates' beliefs about teaching. Borg (2011a) discovered that many of these experienced TESOL teachers were initially unmindful of their beliefs about teaching and learning, but when they were encouraged to articulate and reflect on their meaning, they were better able to note the impact on how they viewed their practice and vice versa but only after a bit of a struggle to be able to state what their beliefs were in the first place. As Borg (2011a: 378) noted within the program, in many cases the in-service TESOL teachers "progressed from an initial stage of limited awareness of their beliefs to feeling quite strongly that they were aware of and could articulate key beliefs underpinning their work." Then as Borg (2011a: 378) observed, the teachers were better able to "develop links between their beliefs and theory."

Wan, Low, and Li (2011) also found that, when in-service TESOL teachers in China were encouraged to articulate and then reflect on their beliefs, but this time through metaphor analysis, it was a transformational experience for them because they were not only able to reappraise them in light of their current practices, but also make modifications to suit their new insight about themselves as TESOL teachers. Wan, Low, and Li (2011) noted that when these in-service TESOL teachers had articulated their beliefs about teaching and learning, they then began to modify their original metaphors, especially if these did not match their newly articulated beliefs. Wan, Low, and Li (2011) observed that when these in-service TESOL teachers were encouraged to reflect on their beliefs through the use of metaphor analysis, this activity enabled them to clearly identify and then clarify their teaching beliefs as they began to reject some of their initial metaphors for teaching because they noted that in reality they diverged from their beliefs. However, Wan, Low, and Li (2011) also noted that although they modified or changed their metaphors, they saw no evidence of changes in their teaching practices.

Principles and Practice

The previous studies for the most part focused on reflections on principles with brief references to practice. However, several of the studies reviewed specifically examined the impact of beliefs on practice and vice versa. Farrell and Bennis (2013) for example, looked at the reflections of two TESOL teachers' (one novice and one experienced) beliefs in Canada and their connections to their actual classroom practices and noted the level of convergence or divergence between both. Similar to the Borg (2011a) study above, they reported that the two experienced TESOL teachers were not consciously aware of the teaching beliefs until they were encouraged to articulate them, but when they did, they realized that these beliefs may not be appropriate to their actual life as a teacher inside and outside the classroom and they thus began to reformulate their beliefs. Farrell and Bennis (2013) observed that when they reflected on their actual classroom practices in light of their newly articulated beliefs, these beliefs tended to diverge more than converge with their actual practices. However, the novice TESOL teacher had more instances of divergence than the more experienced teacher. In terms of actual classroom teaching decisions, in contrast to the novice teacher who, according to Farrell and Bennis (2013: 174), "made instructional decisions based on keeping his students happy," the more experienced teacher tended to make instructional decisions "based on his perceptions of his students' learning." The instances of divergence for the novice teacher were probably as Farrell and Bennis (2013: 173) suggest, because this was the first time the teacher was asked to verbalize these beliefs and therefore it was "possible that he was not sure of his beliefs as they were still in the process of forming." As a result they noted the novice teacher may not have been able to explain why he did what he did in class because he was still trying to articulate and verbalize them to himself. For the more experienced teacher, divergence between beliefs and actual classroom practice was explained by time constraints within a lesson which he said made it difficult for the teacher to put his beliefs fully into practice.

In an interesting contrast to the studies related to in-service TESOL teachers' reflections on principles reported so far, one study reviews how an experienced TESOL teacher in Taiwan, Min (2013), conducted a self-study of her beliefs and practices about how to provide written feedback to her students. By critically examining her beliefs and practices over time in her reflection journal, and learning log, she reported noticeable changes in her guiding principles and underlying beliefs and practices and, as a result, was better able to align her teaching practices with newly articulated beliefs. As Min (2013: 635) observed, "such structural changes in her knowledge and beliefs instigated a substantial change in [practices]." Min (2013: 636) concluded that the teacher's "constant reflection, along with the explicit articulation and demonstration of her beliefs in the form of peer review training, helped align her feedback practices with her beliefs at different points in time." Indeed, this self-study result is a reminder of what Kumaravadivelu (2012: 58) has observed: that one's teaching self is formed by negotiating and making sense of a range of "contemporary realities" and "contradictory expectations" that may be in opposition with a teacher's internal belief or value system and as such the teacher may need to make modifications to both beliefs and practices.

Principles, Theory and Practice

Positive results were also reported when in-service TESOL teachers were prompted to reflect on how their principles intersected with their theory and practice. Best (2011) and Zhoujing (2012) both used action research as a prompt to encourage TESOL teachers to reflect on their principles, theory and practice. In the US, Best (2011) discovered that as a result of their reflections, the TESOL teachers noted that their practices tended to be more grounded in theory. As they became more aware of the connections between all three (principles, theory and practice) though self-monitoring, Best (2011) reported that they were better able to make better theory-practice connections and also made changes in teaching practices because of the greater awareness of these connections. In China, Zhoujing (2012: 25) also used action research to prompt in-service TESOL teachers' reflections because such an approach "addresses theoretical as well as pragmatic issues." Zhoujing (2012: 25) noted that through conducting action research to facilitate such reflection, the TESOL teachers were also better able to make theory-practice connections and as a result "changed themselves, challenging their own routine of thinking." Similar to Best (2011) above, Zhoujing (2012: 26) reported that the TESOL teachers reexamined their beliefs, their students' needs and theory and as a result decided on "action plans and put them into practice."

Also commenting on the transformative power of the impact of articulating beliefs in light of theory and practice, Conway and Denny (2013) reported on results of an in-service course in New Zealand that consisted of a range of reflective activities that included a teaching portfolio. They reported that the TESOL in-service teachers were able to confirm and even modify their beliefs and theories of teaching and learning and come to new understandings of the limitations of their practice with the realizations of refining their teaching approach. Conway and Denny (2013) also observed that the teachers showed development outside their area of focus such as new realizations about the nature and complexities of teaching and learning a second language in general.

Genc (2010: 407) prompted in-service TESOL teachers in Turkey to write a journal in order to explore principles, theory and practice with a specific focus on beliefs about the teaching and learning processes, lesson planning, interaction, classroom management, and assessment. As a result of such reflective writing, Genc (2010: 407) reported that the in-service TESOL teachers "felt empowered and autonomous in their classroom practices when they implemented self-initiated pedagogical options." Because of such reflective writing, Genc (2010) observed that the TESOL teachers were able to develop their own bottom-up view of teaching based on the dynamics of their classrooms. This was, as Genc (2010: 408) noted, "Because they were able to explore, analyze and observe their own beliefs [and theories] and classroom practices, and experiment with alternative instructional behaviors." In a similar approach, Chien (2013: 130) also reported positive results of journal writing to become more aware of and examine "assumptions and beliefs as well as construct knowledge" and improve teaching skills that included "instructional strategies, classroom management issues, and students' English learning and performance."

Farrell (2013a) used analysis of critical incidents as prompts for reflection, because he noted that such an analysis can help in-service TESOL teachers in Canada become aware of discrepancies between principles, theory and practice. When the in-service TESOL teacher in this case study was encourage to recall and describe and then analyze such critical incidents, Farrell (2013a) pointed out that the TESOL teacher began to explore many different assumptions, beliefs and theories that underlie her classroom practices. As the TESOL teacher recalled some critical incidents that were important for her, she gained a greater level of awareness of herself as a TESOL teacher and her underlying beliefs, theory and practices. As Farrell (2013a: 85) observed, by analyzing such critical incidents, especially when outcomes conflict with expectations in those particular incidents, TESOL teachers can come to a greater level of understanding of "what our beliefs, philosophies, understandings, conceptions (of the classroom, of the language, of the students, of ourselves) actually are" rather than what we think they are.

In a more detailed analysis of how teachers can track the changes in beliefs, theory and practice, Farrell (2011a) reported on a short series of classroom observations where an experienced TESOL teacher in Canada used an observation category instrument called SCORE (seating chart observation record) to help her reflect on her classroom practices and how this impacted her theory as well as her teaching beliefs. As Farrell (2011a: 272) observed, "the use of the SCORE instrument enabled the teacher to move from a descriptive reflective phase, where she was able to 'see' the actual communication flow in her class, to a more critical stance on her practice where she could intentionally manipulate the communication flow in a direction she desired." In a similar prompt to the Farrell (2011a) study above, Cutrim Schmid (2011) used video-stimulated reflection as a means for in-service TESOL teachers to reflect on the impact of their beliefs and theory on classroom practices and then evaluate (or re-evaluate) their own overall pedagogical development. As a result, Cutrim Schmid (2011) observed that the TESOL teachers not only had greater access and awareness of their beliefs, theory and practices, but could also track the development of their beliefs, theory and practices as they further developed their capacity for self-reflection and self-evaluation.

Continuing on the theme of tracking changes in teacher beliefs, theory and practice, Phipps and Borg (2009) focused on the relationship between one TESOL teacher's grammar teaching beliefs and classroom practices in Turkey with the aid of post-observation interview and discussions. Phipps and Borg (2009) report that the post-observation discussions helped the TESOL teacher obtain a heightened awareness of the tensions between principles, theory and practice related to grammar teaching, especially when encouraged to attempt alternative classroom teaching practices. As Phipps and Borg (2009: 386) noted:

> It would seem that a crucial factor in enabling her to change her own classroom practice was the awareness of the tension between her stated beliefs and actual practices that was created through the post-lesson discussion of her work. Subsequently trying out alternative practices and subsequently experiencing their benefits first-hand had a powerful influence on her decision to use more group-work in her grammar teaching.

Reflective Questions

- In some cases in-service TESOL teachers are often unaware of their beliefs about teaching and learning. Why do you think this is the case given they have many years of experience teaching?
- If you are an in-service TESOL teacher, are you aware of your beliefs and have you articulated them to yourself or anyone else? If yes, what are they? If no, why not?
- Related to the previous question, why do you think that some in-service TESOL teachers may struggle when attempting to articulate their beliefs about teaching and learning? Did you struggle and if so, why?
- Should an in-service TESOL course help TESOL teachers articulate the key beliefs underpinning their practice? If yes, how can the course do this?
- It was noted in one study that although some in-service TESOL teachers modified or changed their beliefs as a result of their reflections, they made no changes in their teaching practices. Why do you think this was the case?
- One study contrasted the beliefs and practices of a novice TESOL teacher and an experienced TESOL teacher. The study reported that the novice teacher made instructional decisions based on keeping the students happy, but the more experienced teacher made instructional decisions based on the

teacher's perceptions of his students' learning. What is your understanding of this difference and how would you explain the differences?

- Do you agree or disagree with the explanation in the study that for a novice TESOL teacher reflecting on why his or her beliefs diverge from actual classroom practice is because it was the first time the teacher was asked to verbalize these beliefs and therefore it is possible that he was not sure of his beliefs as they were still in the process of forming? Explain your answer.
- Do you agree or disagree with the explanation above that for the more experienced TESOL teacher, divergence between beliefs and classroom practice was explained by time constraints within a lesson which the teacher said made it difficult for him to put his beliefs fully into practice? Explain your answer.
- How can engaging in reflective self-study help a TESOL teacher unlock understanding of assumptions and beliefs and thus transform practice as was reported in one study above?
- Do you think that TESOL teachers should develop their own bottom-up view of teaching based on the dynamics of their classrooms?
- How can recalling and analyzing critical incidents help TESOL teachers get a better understanding of the intersection of beliefs, theory and practice?
- One study reported tensions between TESOL teachers' beliefs, theory and practices. Is it good to have such tensions or should teachers always try to have them all converge? Explain your answer.

Conclusion

This chapter reviewed studies that encouraged pre-service and in-service TESOL teachers to reflect on their principles along with other combinations within the framework for reflecting on practice. Such reflections include explorations of teachers' assumptions, values, beliefs, and conceptions of teaching and learning English as an additional language. The results suggest that most if not all of the studies of both pre-service and in-service TESOL teachers outlined and reviewed were overwhelmingly positive, in that when teachers were encouraged to articulate their beliefs and conceptions of teaching and learning, they were then able to (re)evaluate if these were still appropriate for their current usage. For pre-service TESOL teachers, the results indicate that many of their conceptions of teaching seem to be deeply rooted in their past experiences and when they were able to articulate their underlying assumptions, values, beliefs and conceptions of teaching and learning they were better able to reflect on their appropriateness in light of their current context. As a result, the TESOL pre-service teachers reported that they felt liberated as they became more aware of their own beliefs of language teaching and learning.

In addition, reflections on principles were also combined with other stages of the framework, such as theory and practice, and most studies noted the transformative nature and value of such reflections on beliefs, theory and practices. Many of these reflections resulted in teachers making changes to their practices as well as the other areas but this too created some tension. However, it seems that an important factor enabling teachers to make changes to classroom practice is awareness of the tension between their stated beliefs, theory and actual practices. The results of the chapter suggest that encouraging in-service TESOL teachers to engage in reflective practice beliefs, theory and actual practices with prompts such as discussions, writing, video analysis, critical incident analysis, action research and so on can help TESOL teachers develop awareness of how these all intersect in their classrooms. The next chapter reviews studies related to the practices that encourage TESOL teachers to reflect on their theory of practice.

5

THEORY OF PRACTICE

Introduction

In the previous chapter I outlined and discussed a review of the research when TESOL teachers are encouraged to reflect on their principles of practice as the main focus, and its various combinations with philosophy, theory, practice and beyond practice. In this chapter I proceed with the review to include research that encourages TESOL teachers to reflect where theory of practice is the main focus.

When TESOL teachers are encouraged to reflect on their theory, they explore and examine the different kinds of planning they engage in and the different choices they make about particular skills taught, usually before they teach but also as a result of teaching. Of course these choices are also influenced by their reflections on their philosophy, and their principles as they begin to construct their theory of practice. When TESOL teachers explore and reflect on their theory, this reflection includes the "official" theories they learned in their teacher education programs and courses as well as their "unofficial" theories gained with and from teaching experience. Included in their "unofficial" theories, or "theories-in-use" are the consideration of lesson planning and the different activities and methods teachers choose as they consider the impact of their theory on their practice and the impact of their practice on theory. Another aspect of theory at this third stage of the framework for reflecting on practice is exploration of critical incidents or any unplanned or unanticipated event that occurs during a classroom lesson, which is clearly remembered because it had such a large impact on that teacher. Reflecting on these critical incidents is important because they can be a guide to a teacher's theory building as well as helpful in unearthing the impact of a teacher's philosophy and principles on their theory. Thus, this chapter outlines the research related to pre-service and in-service TESOL teachers' reflections exclusively on theory without any combinations with other aspects of the framework because there were not many studies with such combinations in the review except when in a subordinate role and these combinations are included in another chapter. The review is divided into pre-service TESOL teachers' reflections and this is followed by in-service TESOL teachers' reflections.

Pre-service Teachers' Reflections on Theory

When pre-service TESOL teachers' reflections were exclusively focused on their theory of practice, many of the reviewed studies revealed that the main result of these reflections was the pre-service TESOL teachers' growing awareness of the needs of their students rather than their own need to survive when they took different approaches to planning for teaching. In addition, many of these studies highlighted the use of collaborative lesson planning as a means of encouraging the pre-service TESOL teachers to engage in such reflections.

In a detailed study of the lesson planning process in a TESOL Certificate program in the UK, Morton and Gray (2010) reported that the pre-service TESOL teachers were better able to build their knowledge of instruction and develop different repertoires of instruction as a result of their detailed involvement in lesson planning conferences (LPCs) in which a teacher educator and a group of pre-service TESOL teachers worked together on one particular lesson plan. Morton and Gray (2010) report that when the pre-service TESOL teachers were encouraged to reflect on theory and specifically on planning for teaching through group discussions, they were able to identify important issues related to planning, propose specific actions that would enable successful lessons, evaluate these in light of imagined classroom events. As Morton and Gray (2010: 302) observed, "The LPCs displayed a high degree of recursiveness, in that there were recurrent cycles of identification of problems, searches for solutions, and evaluations of candidate solutions." The recursive nature of such reflections on theory resulted in the pre-service TESOL teachers exercising agency, as Morton and Gray (2010) noted when they identified a problem in the planning process and the teacher educator and pre-service TESOL teachers attempted to find their own solutions; as Morton and Gray (2010: 304) observed, "both TE [teacher educators] and STs [student teachers] were often involved in the search for a solution, with STs quite frequently making suggestions for other STs' action." Thus as Morton and Gray (2010) point out, such collaborative lesson planning conferences (LPCs) and discussions gave the pre-service TESOL teachers the means of extending their questioning of their lesson planning to their existing practices as well as constructing their identity as members of a community of practice of English language teachers, both within the group and also as developing members of the wider community of TESOL teachers.

A number of studies used reflective writing with varying degrees of success, as a means of encouraging pre-service TESOL teachers to reflect on their theory of practice. Tan (2013), for example, explored the written reflections of pre-service

TESOL teachers in Brunei in a teacher education program where the pre-service TESOL teachers were required to observe teaching and then reflect on what they had observed in light of lesson planning and other aspects of teaching as they attended classes weekly on campus. The goal according to Tan (2013: 823) was to create a climate of dialogue where student teachers' professional (and sometimes personal) questions and thoughts were "given due respect and attention" and collectively explored. Specifically, Tan (2013) noted that the pre-service TESOL teachers were encouraged to reflect on topics during their classes that included their planning decisions, classroom management and other pedagogical decisions. Tan (2013: 823) reported that such reflective dialoging (through writing) seemed to help the pre-service TESOL teachers to not only reflect and "talk through" their own reflections on planning and teaching, but also to "understand and see other perspectives" rather than just their own. These other perspectives included an acknowledgment of their students' needs rather than their own needs. As Tan (2013: 823) concluded, such "reflective dialogue is indeed an important, if not essential, component of teacher training and professional development as it can be seen as a means to better understand student teachers' practice, support their efforts and development, and nurture greater reflectivity on the part of all parties."

Wharton (2012) also examined the written reflections of a group of pre-service TESOL teachers in the UK about their experiences of planning and especially their development of teaching materials for future lessons. Specifically, the study wanted to examine the pre-service TESOL teachers' reflections on the benefits of working on materials development with other students through group work and how the participants' understandings of what is involved with materials development evolved, especially if they made changes. However, unlike the results of the Tan (2013) study above, Wharton (2012: 497) reported that for the most part the pre-service TESOL teachers' reflections were mostly of a descriptive nature and thus not very deep or critical and tended to "give an overly positive representation of their experience that was non-critical and negatives were only mentioned to demonstrate resolution." In addition, Wharton (2012: 499) observed that when reflecting on what they perceived as difficult issues, the pre-service TESOL teachers used the group strategically to protect themselves and tended to "associate these difficult issues with the group rather than with themselves alone" as they attempted to save face with any admissions of weakness in their own personal writing.

Sharil and Majid (2010) also looked at reflections of pre-service TESOL teachers in Malaysia as they reflected through writing reflective journals and noted, similar to Wharton (2012), that most of the reflections reported on decisions they made in a descriptive manner rather than giving any reasons why they made such decisions nor did they provide any evaluations of the decisions made. In fact, Sharil and Majid (2010) observed that even though the pre-service TESOL teachers made detailed plans about what they wanted to accomplish in lessons, in practice when these lessons did not go according to their original planning, the pre-service TESOL teachers did not seem to be able to reflect critically on what the issue was because they did not really understand why things did not go according to their original plans. As a result Sharil and Majid (2010) observed they could not even begin to find alternatives so that they could have successful future lessons. As Sharil and Majid (2010: 266) noted, "Even though the participants demonstrated the awareness of having creative approaches in planning, the participants failed to reflect on the 'whys' and 'hows' of their pedagogical planning." Thus most of the pre-service TESOL teachers' reflections on their theory were descriptive non-critical accounts of what occurred; Sharil and Majid (2010: 270) continue, "reasoning was not found to be evident in most of the reflections, and for some that were present, they were not sufficient to explain their decision making."

Sowa (2009: 1028) encouraged pre-service TESOL teachers in the US to reflect through writing but also added the use of action research, and specifically what they called "action research papers" to encourage reflection on theory. Sowa (2009: 1031) reported more positive results than the studies reviewed about as they noted that the pre-service TESOL teachers experienced changes to their understanding about planning and teaching and as a result, were "more open to new and varied [planning and teaching] strategies." Sowa (2009) observed that many of the pre-service TESOL teachers reported becoming more aware of how lesson plans would need some adjustments and how they should be structured to the needs of their students. As Sowa (2009: 1030) remarked, many of the pre-service TESOL teachers "realized they had to have a repertoire of strategies to help meet the needs of all their students, all the time." Sowa (2009) also noted an improved self-efficacy for the pre-service TESOL teachers as they reported that they were able to develop reflective skills needed to investigate their own practice. Thus Sowa (2009: 1031) concluded that "in addition to being more reflective, teachers clearly felt more confident about their teaching, and they exhibited an openness to trying new and varied strategies." In a similar study, Cutrim Schmid and Hegelheimer (2014) also reported positive results with the addition of action research in helping pre-service TESOL teachers in Germany to reflect on their principles, theory and practice as long as the pre-service TESOL teachers are provided with some guidance along the way.

A number of studies that focused on theory used online modes as prompts to encourage pre-service TESOL teachers to reflect, which included online chats, blogs, digital video cases, tele-collaborations and WebCT to name but a few, all of which also reported positive results. For example, taking the idea of collaborative reflections on lesson planning one step further from face-to-face discussions as reported in the Morton and Gray (2010) study above, McLoughlin and Mynard (2009) used online discussions for lesson planning to encourage TESOL teachers in the UAE to reflect. They noted that such a reflective medium with prompts from the instructor not only produced evidence of higher-order thinking skills with greater length and complexity of ideas discussed as compared to their regular face-to-face class discussions, but also allowed the pre-service teachers more time to reflect, and reduced speaking anxiety (see also Farr & Riordan (2012) and Riordan & Murray (2010) studies in Chapter 3).

Tang (2009; 2013) explored blogging as a medium of reflecting on planning lessons, teaching materials and activities and classroom management with pre-service TESOL teachers in Hong Kong. In particular, Tang (2009: 96) examined the use of a blog-based teaching portfolio to encourage reflection of pre-service TESOL teachers and noted that the participants' willingness to share thoughts varied and that participation seemed to be related to group dynamics and effort but all "agreed that they became more reflective after the learning event." Tang (2009) reported that establishing a blog-based portfolio earlier rather than later in a pre-service teacher practicum will allow for greater success in buy-in from the students.

Zottmann, Goeze, Frank, Zentner, Fischer, and Schrader (2012) used a computer-supported case-based learning approach to encourage such pre-service TESOL teachers' reflections on theory in Germany and discovered that in particular digital video cases promoted development of analytical skills of pre-service teachers, but this would need some kind of instructional support as the pre-service teachers could not do this alone.

Dooly and Sadler (2013) attempted to link theory and practice more in a TESOL teacher education program through tele-collaborations in the US and Spain. They attempted to prompt reflection with the idea of linking critical thinking and reflection by integrating technology in the classroom, thus attempting to move from knowledge-telling to knowledge-transforming. Dooly and Sadler (2013) report that such prompts enabled the pre-service TESOL teachers to make more theory-practice connections as well as develop critical thinking and that teacher–teacher lesson planning collaboration resulted in improved lessons.

Parks (2010) used a WebCT discussion forum during a TESL practicum in Canada to help prompt reflection and noted that such a mode of reflection helped the pre-service TESOL teachers to share ideas about planning and teaching and help them become more aware of different perspectives of teaching and learning English. In fact, Parks (2010) reported that the pre-service TESOL teachers were more willing to participate in such Web-based discussions than in face-to-face discussions (see also Morton & Gray, 2010 above) and that they enjoyed reading other pre-service TESOL teachers' posts. Similar to what Morton and Gray's (2010) study reported above, Parks (2010) also noted that the pre-service TESOL teachers felt that they were developing into a community of English teachers. Riordan and Murray (2012), working with pre-service TESOL teachers in Ireland, also report similar conclusions about the highly interactive nature of blogs and chats and note that online discussion forums are more cognitive and that online anonymity may allow for greater openness and willingness to communicate. However, when using both blogs and online forums to encourage reflection on theory, Too (2013), working with pre-service TESOL teachers in Malaysia, cautioned that although both modes allowed for reflection to take place, this reflection was not at the highest level that was transformational, possibly because the teachers preferred to use these communication modes for social rather than cognitive functions (again, I will return to the different modes of reflection in Chapter 8).

Reflective Questions

- How do you plan lessons?
- How can reflecting on theory through collaborative lesson planning for pre-service teachers help them build their knowledge of instruction and develop repertoires of instruction?
- Why would pre-service TESOL teachers need to consider adjusting their lesson plans to the needs of their students and have a repertoire of strategies to help meet the needs of all their students?
- How can online discussions for lesson planning produce evidence of higher-order thinking skills in pre-service TESOL teachers?
- Why would prompts from the instructor be necessary for pre-service teachers when reflecting in online discussions of their theory of practice?
- Why would online reflections on theory allow pre-service TESOL teachers more time to reflect on their theory than face-to-face class discussions?
- Written reflections as a prompt to encourage pre-service TESOL teachers to reflect on their theory seem to have provided mixed results in many of the studies reviewed above, in that most of their reflections are of the descriptive nature and not very critical. Why would this be the case? Would writing need to be linked to other modes of reflection (for example, action research in one study outlined above) and if so, why?
- How can integrating technology in the classroom help pre-service teachers move from knowledge-telling to knowledge-transforming concerning teachers' reflection on theory?
- Why would pre-service TESOL teachers be more willing to participate in such Web-based discussions than in face-to-face discussions about their reflections on theory?

In-service Teachers' Reflections on Theory

When encouraged to articulate and reflect on their theory, for the most part the review of the studies for in-service TESOL teachers reported that they not only realized that they should design their lesson plans in terms of their students' needs but also reported a greater awareness of the possibility of different types of instructional possibilities when preparing their lesson plans. Nishino (2012) for example, looked at in-service TESOL teacher training programs for foreign language teachers in Japan in a program that was specifically aimed at developing communicative language teaching (CLT) in teachers' classrooms. Nishino (2012) remarked that it is important for in-service TESOL teachers to reflect on their theory themselves and how any new theory or approach can be incorporated into parts of their current lessons. Such a level of awareness according to Nishino (2012: 394), "might enable the teachers themselves to design lessons that would fit their teaching contexts, including the use of the new teaching methodology." Thus reflection on theory is important for teachers so that they will be able to design their own lessons, with their own students in mind within their own context. Nishino (2012) also noted that in order to take such reflections on theory one step further it would be necessary for the teachers to design and carry out various demonstration lessons so that they can reflect for themselves how appropriate their lesson planning is. As Nishino (2012: 393) concluded, "Without viewing or taking part in relevant classroom activities, teachers are unlikely to change beliefs that are deeply rooted in their learning experiences."

In addition to reflecting on the design and appropriateness of their lessons for their particular contexts and student needs, when in-service TESOL teachers were encouraged to reflect on their theories, they also reported that they gained a better understanding of their public and personal theories (Wyatt 2010). Wyatt (2010: 256) for instance, looked at an in-service TESOL teacher in Oman who was in a constructivist language teacher further education program that emphasized reflection and where the predominant reflective focus was lesson study, though other reflective practices were also included, such as observation, post-observation conferences, and action research, and noted that the main focus on lesson study reflections helped her develop "considerably as a reflective practitioner." According to Wyatt (2010: 256), the in-service TESOL teacher while examining all aspects of her lesson study and planning was able to draw on her "public as well as personal theories, adapting materials, finding new ideas to experiment with in her classroom and solving problems." At the end of the process, Wyatt (2010) observed that the teacher's discourse indicated that she was becoming more aware of the impact of lesson study on how she performed in the class-room. As Wyatt (2010: 256) noted, at the end of the reflective period process the teacher "possessed reflective qualities and skills, a deep understanding of reflection and the capacity to reflect critically as well as technically." Thus Wyatt (2010) pointed out the importance of such focused in-service TESOL training programs to help develop in-service TESOL teachers' discourse to become more critically reflective about their theory of practice. In a later study Wyatt (2013) also reported on the positive outcomes of how lesson study in an in-service TESOL teacher education program in Oman can promote reflection when attempting to overcome low self-efficacy beliefs when teaching English to young learners. Such reflection together with feedback from a supervisor according to Wyatt (2013: 251), was key to changes in the teacher's [Teacher Self-Efficacy] beliefs in [Teaching English to Young Learners] and "helped her develop both practical knowledge in [Teaching English to Young Learners] and more positive [Teacher Self-Efficacy] beliefs."

Positive outcomes were also reported when in-service TESOL teachers were encouraged to take part in collaborative lesson-planning conferences (Luo, 2014; Shi & Yang, 2014). Shi and Yang (2014) for example, examined the reflections of in-service TESOL teachers while reflecting in collective lesson-planning conferences for a writing course in China. According to Shi and Yang (2014) the main aim of these reflections was to enable the in-service teachers to be able to construct a "shared repertoire" of pedagogical knowledge and practice. As a result of being encouraged to reflect on their lesson planning in such a manner, Shi and Yang (2014: 138) reported that the in-service TESOL teachers, in collaboration with others, were "able to develop a shared understanding of lesson planning." In addition as Shi and Yang (2014: 138) noted, the teachers were able to negotiate "their own views, make meanings applicable to new circumstances, to enlist the collaboration of others, [and] to make sense of events" as they began to get a better understanding of the links between their own theory and practice. By engaging in such collaborative lesson-planning discussions, the in-service TESOL teachers were able to enlist the collaboration of others in order to make sense of events while at the same time asserting their own membership of the community of practice (CoP). In such a community of practice there was a sense of sharing among all the participants and this promoted community cohesion because as Shi and Yang (2014: 139) observed, "The less experienced teachers in the present study were willing to expose their ignorance by asking questions whereas the more experienced were ready to share ideas and their past experiences." As Shi and Yang (2014: 141) remarked, the in-service TESOL teachers said that they had "learned from each other through collective lesson planning" and thus they "helped each other to achieve their common goals," as they "developed their teaching skills."

In a similar result reported by Shi and Yang (2014) above, Luo (2014) also reported the positive effects of collaborative lesson planning to help strengthen the connection between theory and practice for in-service TESOL teachers both "local" English as a foreign language (EFL) teachers and native English speaking teachers (NEST) EFL teachers in elementary schools in Taiwan. As Luo (2014: 406) noted, the in-service TESOL teachers reported that of all the in-service TESOL training they had, the "sessions on collaborative lesson planning [preferred by NESTs] and English language enhancement [preferred by local EFL teachers or NNESTs] were deemed most useful for the teachers." For the NESTs (Luo 2014: 407) who were responsible for most of the lesson planning when engaged in team-teaching situations in elementary schools, and thus had to work with the local teachers, the development of collaborative teaching plans and problem solving and conflict resolution "that could help improve their collaborative teaching performance in elementary schools in Taiwan" were most appreciated. Overall, such collaborations on lesson planning were perceived by all the in-service TESOL teachers according to Luo (2014: 406) as "a context where they could share experiences and learn from other teachers."

In a more detailed account of collaborative lesson planning in China, Xu (2015) also examined the impact of collaborative lesson preparation activities on the professional development of English language teachers and wondered to what extent did the collaborative activities and teacher autonomy have a joint impact on EFL teachers' professional development. Xu (2015: 140) specifically defined collaborative lesson preparation within a China context as "a traditional school-based activity in China in which teachers who teach different classes of the same grade work together to prepare lessons." Such an approach to collaborative lesson preparation can have, as Xu (2015) reports, an overall positive impact of autonomy of in-service TESOL teachers in a teacher development program. In particular, Xu (2015: 146) observed that two types of collaboration emerged from the process of such collaborative lesson preparation: "a product-oriented" type of collaborative lesson preparation where teachers develop an end product for everyone to use: "a complete, ready-to-use set of teaching resources as a visible product which is then shared among its contributors," or a second type of collaborative lesson preparation called a "problem-based" type that mostly featured discussions (either detailed or not). The latter problem-based planning had no final product and so as Xu (2015: 146) noted, with no "help in physical forms," may lead to an increase in teachers' anxiety levels. Thus as Xu (2015) observed, the product-oriented collaborative lesson preparation was more likely to lower teachers' anxiety levels and contribute to a more supportive community environment because they had an agreed end product in hand. Interestingly, though, the study suggested that such lower anxiety levels may not promote teacher autonomy while higher anxiety levels may promote such autonomy because the teachers are more motivated to explore independently, because they realize they need to develop their own lessons themselves. Indeed, Xu (2015) concluded that the level of teacher autonomy depends on the type of collaboration rather than the presence of collaboration.

Similar positive findings of the constructive and promising effects of collaborative lesson-planning were also discovered when online modes of reflection were used to encourage in-service TESOL teachers to engage in collaborative lesson preparation. Wu, Gao, and Zhang (2014) for example, noted that such online discussions on theory for Chinese in-service TESOL teachers were supportive and professionally rewarding, especially for in-service teachers in rural contexts. Murugaiah, Azman, Ya'acob, and Thang (2010) also noted that "discussions" through blogging although time consuming, can create a community of teachers as well as give in-service TESOL teachers in Malaysia an emotional outlet when reflecting on and enhancing skills when preparing lessons in computer assisted language learning (CALL). As Murugaiah, Azman, Ya'acob, and Thang (2010: 79) observed, by being encouraged to engage in such blogging discussions the teachers not only develop their knowledge about teaching but also "get peer support by sharing and collaborating with other members."

Bringing the process of reflecting on theory related to lesson planning one step further, Aliakbari and Bazyar (2012) and Aliakbari and Nejad (2013) reported on the use of team teaching in Iran, where two TESOL teachers plan all the lessons together and teach the same class as a means of encouraging in-service TESOL teachers to reflect on the impact of planning on teaching. Although both studies reported on the advantages of using team teaching, especially for collaborative lesson planning, both studies also noted that such a reflective process could be confusing for some students when the actual lessons are delivered. Aliakbari and Bazyar (2012) for example, examined the effect of team teaching on learners' language proficiency in a type of parallel teaching situation where both teachers assumed full responsibility for planning all the lessons, the presentation of materials, classroom management and student evaluation and discovered that this type of team-teaching approach did not lead to better outcomes than traditional teaching (single teacher instruction). Some reasons Aliakbari and Bazyar (2012) gave for this result was that team teaching caused distractions for some of the students and they found it confusing when two teachers were teaching the same class and this approach had cultural implications related to the context of Iran. Indeed, for the teachers themselves who were engaged in the team teaching, Aliakbari and Bazyar (2012) noted that some said that they felt shy with another teacher in the same room and wondered if both teachers were non-native speakers of English (NNESTs), would they both need to have the same level of language ability and teaching experiences?

In an attempt to address the question posed above about the proficiency level of both NNEST teachers in a team-teaching situation, Aliakbari and Nejad (2013) examined its effect on language proficiency of learners. The team of two in-service TESOL NNEST teachers planned all lessons in advance and specifically co-taught grammar points based on a team-teaching model where both teachers attempted to deliver the grammatical points at the same time with one teacher writing on the board, and the other simultaneously teaching the same structure orally. Aliakbari and Nejad (2013) reported that the team-teaching approach where all lessons were co-planned and co-taught did not contribute to any better results in the grammatical proficiency of the learners than did the single instruction approach where one teacher planned and delivered the complete lesson. Again, as the Aliakbari and Bazyar (2012) study above revealed, Aliakbari and Nejad (2013) remarked that the results may be related to the fact that the students felt confused by such a novel team-teaching approach, because it goes against their cultural expectations of the more acceptable traditional single teacher approach within the Iranian context.

One study was interested in extending the reflective process to include encouraging in-service TESOL teachers to analyze research readings connected to lesson planning as a means of overall continuing professional development (CPD) of the teachers. Kiely and Davis (2010) prompted in-service TESOL teachers in the UK to reflect on and analyze research readings and wondered if the teachers would connect (or even comment on) these readings when discussing lesson planning. Kiely and Davis (2010) reported that the research readings had no real visibility in discussions about lesson planning or classroom analysis and were initially viewed negatively by the participants. However, issues related to teacher identity also appeared in the teachers' discussions, especially when related to discussions on teacher and researcher identities related to TESOL teachers. Kiely and Davis (2010) reported that the teachers were able to draw on a range of theories and concepts in their analysis about their teaching. However, in another cautionary message as above, Kiely and Davis (2010) reported that reflections on theory (lesson planning and delivery) by in-service teachers in a CPD program may influence but not necessarily improve overall teaching practices.

Reflective Questions

- Why would it be important for in-service TESOL teachers to design lessons that would fit their teaching contexts?
- What is your understanding of in-service TESOL teachers' public and personal theories? What are your public theories and what are your private theories (associated with lesson planning)?
- How can teacher educators account for in-service teachers with different levels of experience when prompting them to reflect during collective lesson-planning conferences?
- How can shared lesson-planning conferences help develop community cohesion?
- What are the advantages of collective lesson-planning conferences and how can these help less experienced teachers tap into more experienced teachers' knowledge about lesson planning?
- One study defined collaborative lesson preparation as "a traditional school-based activity in China in which teachers who teach different classes of the same grade work together to prepare lessons." Do you agree or disagree with this definition? If yes, why? If not, provide your definition.
- What is your understanding of the two types of collaborative lesson preparation that emerged in one study of lesson-planning conferences: *product-oriented* collaboration and *problem-based* collaboration?
- One type of the collaborative lesson planning models listed in the above question tended to lower anxiety levels but this may not promote teacher autonomy, while the other led to higher anxiety levels and this may promote such teacher autonomy. What is your understanding of this?
- What are the advantages and disadvantages of a team-teaching approach to reflecting on lesson planning and delivery?
- Why would students become confused with a team-teaching approach?
- How would you plan and execute a team-teaching series of lessons?
- In a team-teaching situation where both teachers were non-native speakers of English (NNESTs), would they both need to have the same level of language ability and teaching experiences?

- Why would, as one study reported, reflections on theory (lesson planning and delivery) by in-service teachers in a CPD program influence but not necessarily improve overall teaching practices?

Conclusion

This chapter reviewed studies that encouraged pre-service and in-service TESOL teachers to reflect on their theory. Although the focus of the chapter was solely on theory (and thus did not use combinations because they are, or will be, covered in other chapters), there were instances where it was not possible to separate the impact of some other stages of the framework and as such these were mentioned. Overall though the results suggest that most, if not all, of the studies of both pre-service and in-service TESOL teachers outlined and reviewed were overwhelmingly positive in that when teachers were encouraged to explore and reflect on their theory through lesson planning, they had positive experiences. For pre-service TESOL teachers, collaborative lesson planning and preparation seemed to lead them to realize the importance of focusing on the needs of their students so that they could approach and plan lessons using different approaches as they developed their repertoire of teaching skills. For in-service TESOL teachers, reflecting on their theory through collaborative lesson planning and preparation (face-to-face and online) also seemed to yield positive outcomes. The results of many studies suggest that the in-service teachers not only became more aware of their lesson planning details but also, as a result of this awareness, realized the possibility of different types of instruction and the importance of context when planning lessons as well as when attempting collaborations through team-teaching situations. One study concluded that a reflective focus on theory alone may not necessarily lead to improvements in overall practice. The next chapter, reflections on practice, will cover this issue in more detail for both pre-service and in-service TESOL teachers.

6

PRACTICE

Introduction

In the previous chapter I outlined and discussed a review of the research when TESOL teachers are encouraged to reflect exclusively on their theory of practice. In this chapter I proceed to review research that encouraged TESOL teachers to reflect on their practice, the next stage of the framework. However, there were no clear instances where the teachers just focused their reflections on their practice exclusively without combining these reflections with other aspects of the framework such as practice and theory in a subordinate role (hence I did not cover this in the previous chapter). In this chapter the focus will be on reflections on practice and especially how it is combined with reflections on theory. Examples of when practice was combined with other stages of the framework are covered in other chapters because it was deemed that the main focus of the reflections was the other stages, such as philosophy and practice (see Chapter 3), principles and practice (see Chapter 4), or beyond practice (see Chapter 7).

When TESOL teachers are encouraged to reflect on their practice, they explore and examine the more visible aspect of their work, namely their actual teaching. Most of what a TESOL teacher does before he or she enters the classroom to practice, however, is not as easily visible and as such goes unnoticed by many who are not related to the teaching profession. Thus reflecting on practice starts with an analysis of observable actions a TESOL teacher makes in a classroom while teaching a lesson and includes what he or she says and does and how the students react or do not react. Such actions involve the teacher thinking while doing the action, some before the teacher does or says anything, or reflection for action, while others are after the teacher says or does something, or reflection on action. During all these moments teachers can be encouraged to reflect on their overall practice.

When teachers engage in reflection-*in*-action they attempt to consciously stand back while they are teaching as they monitor and adjust to various circumstances that are happening within the lesson. When teachers engage in reflection-*on*-action they are examining what happened in a lesson after the event has taken place and this is a more delayed type of reflection than the former. When teachers engage in reflection-*for*-action they are attempting to reflect before anything has taken place and anticipate what may happen and try to account for this before they conduct the lesson. Many of the decisions a teacher makes, the actions he or she performs or what the teacher gets his or her students to do can be informed and influenced by his or her theory and planning before he or she enters the room or as a result of a previous lesson. This chapter thus outlines and appraises the research related to pre-service and in-service TESOL teachers' reflections on practice and especially how this is combined with their theory. The review is divided into pre-service teachers and this is followed by in-service TESOL teachers.

Pre-service Teachers' Reflections on Practice

As mentioned above, the main focus of pre-service TESOL teachers' reflections was practice and theory because no studies focused solely on practice, which makes sense, as teachers just do not teach without any plans, either written or in their head, before they enter the classroom. The closest linkage on the framework is theory or the details of planning and its impact on practice, with practice featuring most in the results of the studies reviewed.

Studies that encouraged pre-service TESOL teachers to reflect on their practice and planning without much mentorship (i.e., they were just asked to write or talk about their reflections) reported that the teachers did not move much beyond descriptive reflection and engaged in a lot of self-blame as they focused mostly on their own behavior and little on their students' learning.

Yesilbursa (2011a,b) examined TESOL pre-service teachers' written reflections in Turkey after they watched their own video-recorded microteaching lessons as well as the patterns that emerged from these reflections in terms of descriptive and dialogic reflection. The results were somewhat unclear as Yesilbursa (2011a, b) discovered that generally such reflection was largely only descriptive in nature when they focused on practice as they did not really explore the impact of their planning on their practices nor did they make changes to their planning or teaching as a result of their reflections. Specifically, Yesilbursa (2011b) reported that although many of the pre-service TESOL teachers may have approached such reflection in unique and individual ways, and as a result gained a high academic grade within their teacher education courses, this high grade was not translated into high teaching performance when the pre-service teachers were encouraged to reflect on the impact of their planning on their teaching and vice versa; as Yesilbursa (2011b: 179) concluded, "high academic performance may not always entail practical expertise or the potential for creative reflection with an open mind." This conclusion, although acknowledged by many teacher educators and teachers alike, has not been given enough attention in the language teacher education literature. I return to this issue in the overall appraisal chapter (Chapter 9).

Tavil (2014) similarly used writing, but this time electronic journals (or e-journals), to prompt pre-service TESOL teachers in South Africa to reflect on their self-efficacy. As a result, Tavil (2014) observed that the pre-service TESOL teachers increased their reflective abilities, became better problem-solvers, and developed more self-confidence and better instructional strategies which led to increased student achievement in their lessons. It is interesting to note here that Tavil (2014) also had a group of pre-service TESOL teachers who reflected in general about their self-efficacy but did not use e-journaling as a mode of reflection. Tavil (2014) reported that this second group of TESOL teachers did not see any significant change in their self-efficacy nor was there any change reported in their ability to reflect critically on their practice.

Cabaroglu (2014) added action research to journal writing as a means of fostering reflection on practice among pre-service TESOL teachers in Turkey and also reported positive impact on self-efficacy of the teachers. As Cabaroglu (2014: 84) remarked, there was a "highly significant increase in student teachers' reported self-efficacy beliefs from Time 1 (before they were engaged in action research) and Time 2 (after the completion of action research projects)." This "promoted reflective learning and deep thinking." As a result, the pre-service teachers saw a big improvement in their problem-solving skills and noted a big improvement in their teaching.

Kömür and Çepik (2015) were interested in having pre-service TESOL teachers in Turkey reflect on their daily life routines and experiences through journal writing outside of contact hours for the course on learning and teaching. More specifically, they wrote about their first experience of conducting lessons in an actual school classroom and shared that they found it exciting and rewarding. The teachers were also given feedback on their reflections and as a result pointed out some specifics that they learned in these lessons, such as the importance of using visual aids and real-life activities in the classroom in order to increase students' participation in language-learning activities. They also noted their insecurities with classroom management in these lessons and their fear of making mistakes and soon realized the need to use a variety of materials in the classroom to encourage students to participate in the learning process more actively in order to minimize classroom management problems. As a result of their reflections on their teaching practice, the pre-service TESOL teachers expressed a concern about the inconsistency between theory provided in teacher education programs and actual experiences of practice. So they highlighted a need for more practice in the methodology courses in their teacher education program. Such reflections have implications for TESOL teacher education courses and I return to this issue again in Chapter 9.

Zhu (2014) examined the nature of reflection of pre-service TESOL teachers in China when they focused their reflections on classroom discourse during their practicum training. Zhu (2014) reported that they focused mostly on physiological and pedagogical aspects of classroom discourse but not on sociocultural and interpersonal aspects of classroom discourse. Regarding the physiological aspects, Zhu (2014) observed that they wrote mostly about problems such as their low voice, their multiple repetitions, grammar mistakes and unclear instructions. Zhu (2014: 1280) stated that the pre-service TESOL teachers' reflections, especially when it came to problem judgment, were "dependent on authorities" rather than collecting any real evidence themselves, and then they tried to come up with spontaneous solutions to the problem. As Zhu (2014: 1280) states, although the pre-service TESOL teachers were eager to improve their teaching, their journal entries were "full of self-blame as they put too much focus on their own behavior," which leads to anxiety. As Zhu (2014) noted, because of their lack of experience and lack of teaching schemata, the pre-service teachers did not reflect deeply and did not know how to quickly deal with any unexpected problems. Zhu (2014) concluded that it is important that pre-service TESOL teachers have some mentorship and guidance (as the results of the studies reviewed above concur) so that they can become more critical and independent reflective thinkers in the classroom.

Moser, Harris, and Carle (2012) were more successful in encouraging pre-service TESOL teachers in Japan to make some changes in their teaching when they engaged in a special "teacher-talk training course" in which they recorded and reflected on their own teacher talk while they were teaching. The pre-service TESOL teachers compared their own teacher talk before and after task performances. Although the pre-service teachers said that initially they felt uncertain, and confused about what they were doing, once they got over the embarrassment of hearing their own voices, many according to Moser, Harris, and Carle (2012: 86) reported that "hearing their performances helped them improve prosodic features of their speaking." It may be then that encouraging pre-service TESOL teachers to reflect in a more focused manner on a specific item in their teaching repertoire such as teacher talk may be better than just asking them to reflect on their teaching and planning in a general manner. As Moser, Harris, and Carle (2012: 87) commented on the effects of such specific training, "We tried to demonstrate to teachers that even with limited proficiency they could, through proper planning and preparation, conduct successful communicative lessons."

Up to this point the review has noted, with regard to encouraging pre-service TESOL teachers to reflect on their practice and theory, that some of the studies reviewed above report mixed results regarding the development of critical reflection when pre-service TESOL teachers are left to conduct these reflections on their own without any guidance and/or these reflections are not focused on a particular aspect of their practice. However, whenever guidance and feedback, even of a general nature, are provided, studies show that the pre-service TESOL teachers seemed to make clearer connections between theory and practice. Thus it seems that some form of intervention may be necessary to help pre-service TESOL teachers to move from descriptive to critical reflections when exploring the influence of planning on practice and vice versa. The following studies reviewed below suggest that pre-service TESOL teachers may benefit from such an intervention that provides feedback of some kind that can take many different forms, such as with peers, teacher educators, mentors, and/or supervisors. The following reviewed studies attest to this.

Waring (2013) examined what prompted reflections in post-observation conferences between practicum course instructor and pre-service TESOL teachers in the US. Waring (2013: 114) reported that feedback given by the mentor-teacher in such post-observational conferences is very important because it "can function as triggers for teacher reflections." This is because, as Waring (2013: 114) suggests, when the mentor gives feedback, the pre-service teacher, when accepting or rejecting, "engages a range of reflective talk such as articulating an independent analysis of her success, reconsidering a pedagogical practice, or relating her difficult endeavors in effectuating a certain behavioral change." It is this act of accepting or rejecting that causes the pre-service teacher to reflect on his or her reasoning and considering alternative courses of action to continue or change approaches. Thus, the mentor-teacher's prompts are very important according to Waring (2013: 115), "for nurturing the possibilities of reflection."

Taking the idea of prompts further in order to trigger more critical reflection in such post-observation conferences, Waring (2014) examined specific actions mentor-teachers or supervisors can take to avoid too many general comments with pre-service TESOL teachers in the US. When probing for reflections on issues, Waring (2014) suggests the mentor-teacher or supervisor prioritize the pre-service TESOL teachers' perspectives so as to invite reflection and thus take a solution-attentive approach rather than a cause-attentive approach, because the latter can put the pre-service teacher on the defensive rather than fostering a real understanding of the issue. Because pre-service TESOL teachers use such discussions for defending themselves or displaying their competence as prospective teachers, mentor-teachers must be aware of their avoidance of making connections between problems observed and their own practice and thus engage in lower levels of reflection. As Waring (2014: 117) has noted, it is difficult to escape the "testing" aspect of these power dynamics and "as such, although the teachers do treat the mentor questions as eliciting reflection, they can approach answering with great caution, orienting to any noticing preceding the question and the question itself as incipient critiques." Thus, mentor-teachers can provide prompts by asking specific and focused questions in a solution-attentive approach that better scaffolds teacher learning and enables deeper reflections.

Mirici and Hergüner (2015) took the idea of assessment mentioned above by Waring (2013, 2014) further when examining the impact of Turkish pre-service TESOL teachers' use of the European Portfolio for Student Teachers of Languages (EPOSTL) as a self-assessment tool. The main aims of the EPOSTL are, among others, to encourage pre-service teachers to reflect on their competences and on the underlying knowledge which feeds this competence. Other aims include the promotion of discussions among pre-service teachers, their peers, and teacher educators and mentors, as well as to facilitate self-assessment of pre-service TESOL teachers' competences. The idea is that the EPOSTL is an instrument which can help chart the progress of pre-service teachers. Mirici and Hergüner (2015) reported that the EPOSTL provided the pre-service TESOL teachers time and space for reflection on their achievements and it gave them the opportunity to regularly track their own progress and to determine individual goals for their own learning situations.

Arshavskaya and Whitney (2014: 732) also noted the critical role of the supervisor in mediating a novice's learning-to-teach in the US when encouraged to reflect using a dialogic blog in order to enhance the novice teacher's understanding of teaching and help her apply "those understandings in her actual practice." As a result of using a dialogic blog, Arshavskaya and Whitney (2014: 732) report that the teacher moved from "simply receiving mediation from the supervisor to eliciting and engaging mediation from the supervisor as well as from her mentor teacher and peers." This underscores the critical role of the supervisor in mediating the learning process according to Arshavskaya and Whitney (2014) because such dialogic exchanges between the supervisor and pre-service teacher develop her teaching expertise over time.

Golombek and Doran (2014) looked at how dialogic journal reflections can orient teacher educators in mediating novice language teachers' professional development, and especially they noted the pervasiveness of emotional content in one pre-service TESOL teacher's journal. Golombek and Doran (2014: 110) observed that such journal writing enable the teacher educator to gain insight into the novice teacher's thinking, feeling and doing of teaching and the teacher was generally receptive to "the mediation she received." Such a process according to Golombek and Doran (2014: 110) "enabled the teacher educator to mediate each journal entry synchronically and diachronically to explore the emotional dissonance identified, to provide appropriate mediation in response, and to calibrate mediational responses in reaction to the next round of Josie's [the novice teacher] journal responses." Golombek and Doran (2014) concluded that the pre-service TESOL teacher's emotions are part of her normal development as a teacher and indeed can be a valuable resource to be incorporated into each teacher's professional development.

Engin (2015) also looked at the role written documents (rather than dialogue/ discussion) can play to encourage pre-service TESOL teachers in Turkey to reflect during post-observation feedback sessions in order to try to maximize the learning and as Engin (2015: 263) observed, develop a sense of "co-construction of meaning between mentor and pre-service TESOL teachers" similar to the conclusions of Golombek and Doran (2014) above. Engin (2015: 263) discovered that such written commentary between pre-service TESOL teachers and a teacher educator was important because it not only provided "a written, tangible and permanent account of the lesson" but also played a central role in post-observation feedback sessions because it acted as "a catalyst for discussion and reflection."

However, one constraint of using written artifacts as a platform for pedagogic conversations about practice that Engin (2015) noted is the issue of power relations, in that the teacher educator has sole authority when filling it in. As Engin (2015: 264) cautioned, "Since the tutor has filled in the artefact, and has sole access to it, then the discourse will inevitably be controlled by the tutor in terms of what to discuss, in what order and through which questions."

One way around the issue of power relations and the development of dependency on a supervisor/teacher educator/mentor is the use of video-recording, according to Eröz-Tuğa (2012), as a means of developing more independence and critical reflection on practice. Eröz-Tuğa (2012) examined how self-reflection through discussion of video-recorded teaching sessions can lead to the development of a critical perspective into classroom practices because such video-recording feedback sessions are less dependent on peers and supervisor for feedback and reflection. Eröz-Tuğa (2012) reported positive effects of such video-recording and feedback sessions as the pre-service TESOL teachers became more aware of their own strengths and weaknesses of their practice as well as improved ability to provide insightful and constructive comments. The pre-service teachers also reported that they felt more empowered and motivated as prospective teachers. Akcan (2010) examined Turkish pre-service TESOL teacher candidates' opinions about their teaching performance after they also watched themselves on video with the university supervisor in interactional feedback sessions and came to a similar conclusion as Eröz-Tuğa (2012). Such sessions according to Akcan (2010) led to heightened awareness of teaching practices among the pre-service teachers as they identified their strengths and weaknesses and developed a more critically reflective stance towards their practice.

In a more elaborate development of the use of visuals as prompts to encourage pre-service TESOL teachers to develop a critically reflective stance on their practice, Kozlova and Priven (2015) took to the virtual world in order to encourage pre-service TESOL teachers in Canada to reflect on their lesson planning and teaching practice and reported positive outcomes in terms of the development of critical reflection on theory and practice. Using such virtual worlds with the ability for text, audio and video chat, pre-service TESOL teachers took a course on teaching ESL in 3D virtual worlds with sessions that were in two stages, a pre-teaching stage which consisted of lesson study and discussion, and a teaching stage which consisted of observation of each other's teaching followed by post-observation conferences. Kozlova and Priven (2015: 98) noted the positive aspects of feedback provided by peers and teacher educator as they observed that "throughout the project, teacher trainees were able to incorporate peers' suggestions and borrow peers' ideas when developing tasks on wikis, to providing feedback and incorporating peers' feedback during the dry runs." Kozlova and Priven (2015: 98) also observed that such a process of collaboration with the use of 3D technology provided a means for the pre-service teachers "to critically reflect on their own teaching sessions ... and to make necessary changes to their tasks after observing peers' teaching sessions."

Other studies have complemented this use of 3D technology and video recordings as prompts for post-observation reflection by forms of peer group discussion and/or feedback from critical friends. Hepple (2012) for example, examined the reflections of pre-service TESOL teachers in Hong Kong on a teaching episode which was video-recorded followed immediately by a focus group discussion analyzing aspects of the teaching experience, which was also recorded. First, working in pairs, the pre-service teachers were engaged in teaching a cultural task to a small group of students in one lesson. The second phase consisted of the teaching pair discussing their perception of the teaching experience via a stimulated recall interview with the lecturer, one week after conducting the teaching task. Hepple (2012) observed that such a process of peer directed discussions enabled the pre-service teachers to begin to articulate their pedagogical understandings, although not at a deep, critically reflective level. As Hepple (2012: 319) noted, the pre-service TESOL teachers "did not move from identifying their pedagogy to critically questioning this." Similar to what Waring (2013, 2014) concluded above, Hepple (2012: 319) noted that in order for the pre-service TESOL teachers to become more deeply reflective, they would need prompts from the supervisor "as a trusted third party listener in a privileged position to take up this catalytic role" and this can be accomplished through scaffolding and stimulated recall techniques. As Hepple (2012: 319) has noted, "without exposing their assumptions and viewpoints to critical review, the participants are unlikely to develop new understandings and reformulate their practice."

Nguyen and Baldauf (2010) reported positive effects of the use of peer mentoring sessions with pre-service TESOL teachers in Vietnam in a practicum to encourage reflections, and especially when these sessions were formally structured with the help of the teacher educator. As Nguyen and Baldauf (2010: 54) observed, there was evidence of "a significant change in scores related to instructional practice as evaluated by the school mentors and the university supervisors between the participants who were involved in the mentoring training intervention and the participants who participated in the ordinary program." Nguyen and Baldauf (2010) concluded that peer mentoring can help pre-service TESOL teachers to develop more robustly during the practicum. One of the reasons that made this improvement possible as cited in a follow-up study by Nguyen (2013) in the same context was the development of support and trust between all the participants as a result of such mentoring. Such support according to Nguyen (2013) consisted of emotional support, as the teachers began to share all aspects of their lives as well as talk openly to each other and this led to the creation of a community group spirit. As Nguyen (2013: 40) observed, such a "group provides a high level of psychosocial support." Gan (2014) also reported similar positive results with the use of peer mentoring in fostering a sense of sharing among fellow pre-service TESOL teachers in Hong Kong. As Gan (2014: 136) remarked, for the pre-service teachers "the timely feedback of peers contributed to valuing of personal experience in capacity to generate knowledge for teaching."

However, not all peer mentoring relationships reported such positive results. Wachob (2011) cautioned about the importance of considering context when implementing peer mentoring. When encouraging pre-service TESOL teachers in Egypt as participants in Critical Friend Circles (CFC) to provide feedback on practice, Wachob (2011) observed that the most important challenge was the issue of cultural sensitivity, as the pre-service TESOL teachers struggled at times when they had to give and receive critical feedback. As Wachob (2011: 365) remarked, the "first challenge is to understand that Egyptian culture does not readily accept the concept of cool feedback in public." As a result, Wachob (2011) speculated that the reasons the pre-service TESOL teachers were defensive, hesitant and hedging their comments was that they wanted to avoid any personal conflicts within their existing friendships. Thus the participants repeatedly provided "warm feedback" to each other so that they could avoid what they perceived to be culturally inappropriate. According to Wachob (2011: 365), this then led to other challenges such as how to give feedback, what protocols to use as a guide for the participants as well as encouraging them to use "the reflection techniques to continue their own professional development." However, Wachob (2011) reported that eventually the pre-service teachers came to value such critical friendships and noted that the positives outweighed the negatives as the participants perceived them as beneficial because they enhanced their critical thinking skills, and prompted self-reflection that led to improved teaching.

Reflective Questions

- One study of TESOL pre-service teachers' reflections on the impact of their planning on their teaching and vice versa did not yield much in terms of teaching or planning changes and the author concluded that high academic performance in teacher education courses may not always entail practical expertise or the potential for creative reflection when it comes to teaching. Why do you think this would be the case?
- When pre-service TESOL teachers are reflecting on their actual classroom teaching why do they usually (and only) focus on themselves as teachers and their perceptions of negative aspects of their teaching such as was reported in one study above: problems such as their low voice, their multiple repetitions, grammar mistakes and unclear instructions?
- Why would it be important for pre-service TESOL teachers to also focus on the positive aspects of their teaching?
- Do you think that encouraging pre-service TESOL teachers to reflect in a more focused manner on a specific item in their teaching repertoire (such as teacher talk in the study reviewed above) may be better than just asking them to reflect on their teaching and planning in a general manner?

- Some pre-service TESOL teachers expressed a concern about the inconsistency between theory provided in teacher education programs and actual experiences of practice. Why do you think this would be the case and have you experienced this?
- Many studies reviewed suggest that some form of feedback or guidance from a supervisor as well as discussions of some kind in post-observation conferences with teacher educators, mentors, supervisors and/or peers may be important to foster critical reflection. Why is this?
- What is your understanding of the idea that a mentor-teacher or supervisor should take a "solution-attentive approach" rather than a "cause-attentive approach" when providing feedback?
- When pre-service TESOL teachers get feedback from supervisors, one study noted is the issue of power relations, in that the teacher educator has sole authority in deciding the form and content of reflection to a certain extent. How can such power relations impact a pre-service TESOL teacher's reflections on practice?
- One way around power relations and the development of dependency on a supervisor/mentor/teacher educator that has been suggested is the use of video-recording feedback sessions to free the pre-service TESOL teacher. Do you agree with this and if so how can video sessions encourage more critical reflection?
- Peer mentoring was incorporated in many studies as a means of fostering sharing among pre-service TESOL teachers when reflecting on their practice and theory. However, one study noted the challenge of context when incorporating such peer mentoring modes of reflection. What is your understanding of this issue?

In-service Teachers' Reflections on Practice

When in-service TESOL teachers were encouraged to reflect on practice in combination with theory, many studies reviewed reported the importance of self-monitoring and the usefulness of classroom observations to aid reflection, and similar to results of the studies reviewed above for pre-service TESOL teachers, issues related to usefulness of feedback provided either by peers or facilitators seemed to be the focus of many of these studies. In addition, many studies also reported on the usefulness of action research as a prompt for encouraging reflection for in-service TESOL teachers on practice and theory.

In terms of self-monitoring as a form of reflection on practice, Fahim, Hamidi, and Saremb (2013) examined the impact of heightened self-monitoring on Iranian in-service TESOL teachers' reflections on their students' comments about their teaching and their willingness to alter their teaching practices in order to meet the stated needs of their students. Fahim, Hamidi, and Saremb (2013) reported that when teachers engaged in self-monitoring and reflected on their teaching methodologies and perceived problems of their students, they said that they became better educators and this was transferred to their teaching practices because it resulted in the better performance of their students (in this case their willingness to communicate more in classes).

Mercado and Baecher (2014) also explored self-monitoring with in-service TESOL teachers in Peru and specifically video-based self-observation as a prompt for individual, reflective practice. They noted that the teachers were able to identify their strengths and weaknesses as a result of their heightened awareness of the classroom environment and their teaching practices and this awareness eventually led to changes to their actual classroom practices. Mercado and Baecher (2014) reported that self-observation through video was the primary catalyst for promoting self-monitoring, self-assessment, and self-reflection, all of which eventually led to improving teaching effectiveness and student learning.

Kang and Cheng's (2013) case study examined how classroom practices of an in-service TESOL teacher in China can change over time as a result of engaging in self-reflection that included lesson study (theory) and classroom observations. Initially, though, Kang and Cheng (2013) observed that the in-service TESOL teacher was not initially interested in reflecting, but as she began to reflect and "see" her own teaching in a different manner, she began to experiment for herself and developed a more positive attitude towards such systematic reflections. Such reflective processes, according to Kang and Cheng (2013: 179), provided the teacher with "an opportunity to articulate her thinking behind decision-making, evaluate the efficacy of teaching, compare alternatives of practices, and finally change her classroom behaviors." As a result, Kang and Cheng (2013: 182) reported that "Thanks to the reflection on alternative ways of teaching, [the teacher was] empowered to expand her pedagogical choices ... changes in cognition led to changes in behavior and changes in behavior led to changes in cognition."

The inclusion of classroom observations to encourage TESOL teachers to engage in self-monitoring and self-reflection also raised the issue of the affective component of reflecting on one's practice. Lasagabaster and Sierra (2011) questioned in-service TESOL teachers in Spain about their thoughts and beliefs towards classroom observations in order to see if such a reflective component is linked to positive feelings or negative feelings by in-service TESOL teachers. Lasagabaster and Sierra (2011: 454) reported that most of the teachers said that they perceived that classroom observation is "important because it enhanced awareness," because it allows teachers to compare ideas about their lesson planning and actual classroom practices which can lead to greater awareness of different types of instruction. However, Lasagabaster and Sierra (2011: 454) also observed that some of the teachers may not always have been truthful in their replies because they "didn't want to be negative or critical of the other teacher." In addition, in terms of the affective component of classroom observations, Lasagabaster and Sierra (2011: 456) further reported that "the most frequent reactions from those averse to being watched were uneasiness, distrust, insecurity and anxiety about having an observer in class with them."

In a similar study to Lasagabaster and Sierra (2011) above, Ryder (2012) also wondered about the affective side of observations for in-service TESOL teachers in France when invited to engage in classroom observations as part of their reflections on practice and discovered two different types of responses. The first response was negative, because according to Ryder (2012: 180), the teachers saw no need to participate in any classroom observations when encouraged to reflect on their practice because the said that "they felt no need for help" and anyway said that they had no time to set them up. As such they did not engage in any classroom observations as part of their reflections on practice. The second response was more positive and those in-service TESOL teachers that did participate remarked that they thought it would be good for career advancement and professional status rather than for any overall reflective rewards and this may have been because they were all contract teachers according to Ryder (2012). However, Ryder (2012) also observed that these same teachers reported that classroom observations were also important for them because they said they were interested in meeting the needs of learners and especially how to teach unmotivated students. Ryder (2012) also reported that for those who participated in classroom observations, some teachers showed evidence of behavior changes but other teachers did not make any changes. The results of the above studies indicate that when teachers are encouraged to reflect through classroom observations, the affective side of this mode of reflection needs to be addressed in order to take into account teachers' feelings about being observed and about giving and receiving feedback.

This issue of feedback was the focus of other studies that examined feedback provided by peers, either in pairs as critical friends or in study groups, as well as feedback from facilitators as prompts for reflection. Arslan and Ilin (2013) for example, noted the positive impact of in-service TESOL teachers in Turkey discussing practice with peers especially as it relates to the important issue of classroom management. Arslan and Ilin (2013) examined the impact of a short peer-coaching activity where teachers were in pairs and observed one another's lessons, exchanged feedback and repeated the process at a later time. Such a process of peer discussions allowed collaboration between the pairs and resulted in changes in teaching related to classroom management because it was tailored to their individual needs, a point noted by Farrell (2001) some years ago.

Shousha (2015: 135) examined the perceptions of in-service TESOL teachers in Saudi Arabia towards peer observation in which the teachers themselves "developed the peer observation protocol, agreed on a record form for the class visit and an instrument for evaluation of teaching to be used as a guide during the observation." Shousha (2015) noted that many of the teachers cited challenges such as time, work load, lack of constructive feedback from colleagues because of fear of offending them, and the completion of various forms as formidable impediments to such observations. Although most teachers reported that they increased their self-confidence as a result of peer observation, Shousha (2015: 139) suggested that for peer observation to be successful as a means of prompting reflection there is a "need for simplification [that] reflects the need of some teachers to have more clarification of and training on the items used in the checklist."

Lakshmi (2014) noted that when encouraged to reflect on their theory and practice, the in-service TESOL teachers in India sought the advice of their senior colleagues in the group when reflecting on their classroom issues." This process encouraged the teachers to try out alternative teaching practices while making informed decisions about these practices. As a result of such discussions, Lakshmi (2014: 202) reported that the teachers "became more empowered as they developed a sense of self as teacher which brought a new sense of meaning and significance to their classroom work." Although the teachers noted that the process was time consuming, they realized such reflections allowed them to gain a deeper understanding of their practices so that they could decide on alternative practices when warranted.

Gun (2010) also noted the positive impact of systematic reflections especially when teachers discuss these with colleagues rather than just watching their own video-recorded lessons by themselves. Gun (2010) working with in-service TESOL teachers in Turkey observed that such a reflective process which involved feedback from colleagues was social, friendly and involved sharing, empathizing and understanding and helped the teachers become autonomous.

Vo and Mai Nguyen (2010) used critical friend discussions with in-service TESOL teachers in Vietnam and similar to what Shousha (2015) above discovered, the participants were initially hesitant to offer any criticism to others in the group for fear of offending them. This reluctance diminished, however, as they became more trusting of each other. In the end, Vo and Mai Nguyen (2010: 210) observed that the critical friends created "opportunities to exchange professional ideas, opportunities to learn from colleagues" and "the development of good work relationships and a professional community." The result of these reflections with critical friends according to Vo and Mai Nguyen (2010), was that it allowed the teachers to develop a sense of community and even improve their teaching, as they learned from one another's reflections on their teaching.

Mak and Pun (2015) report on a series of planned efforts on cultivating a group of in-service TESOL teachers in Hong Kong into a community of practice (CoP) where teachers could learn from each other. Mak and Pun (2015: 18) observed that although there were some initial tensions when forging individual and group identity "arising out of different personalities and/or backgrounds," they eventually managed to develop and work as a group by putting aside many of their individual concerns. As Mak and Pun (2015: 18–19) remarked: "The coalescing of these individual idiosyncrasies came up with some group synergy that enabled individual teachers to find, establish, discover, and develop their expertise-in-self in the process." Mak and Pun (2015) concluded that for groups working on their own to develop knowledge about their practice, it is up to individual teachers to have an open mind when it comes to recognizing and absorbing differences in approaches to practice.

Perhaps then as Hung and Yeh (2013) propose, such critical friends and group reflections may best be facilitated and more beneficial to all concerned and especially if the participants are reluctant to provide feedback for fear of offending when they are guided by a facilitator. Hung and Yeh (2013) looked at the reflections of in-service TESOL teachers in Taiwan in bi-weekly group meetings with the help of a facilitator and reported that the group discussions enabled the teachers to share their practical knowledge with each other, co-design various teaching activities and engage in self-appraisal of their classroom teaching. As Hung and Yeh (2013: 163) noted, the teachers "gradually gained autonomy over their learning and made efforts to integrate what they learned [about *theory/practice* connections] into their own classrooms." However, Hung and Yeh (2013: 163) also maintain that some kind of stimulus must be provided by an experienced facilitator "in engaging teachers [no matter how experienced] in the learning process and bringing about changes in their beliefs and classroom practices." As Hung and Yeh (2013: 163) report: "even the teachers with many years of teaching experience still needed stimulus and support to promote their continuous learning." Thus it seems that when groups of teachers come together to reflect on their theory and practice and given that many in the group will have different levels of experience and personalities, the use of an experienced facilitator may be necessary to stimulate reflection in order to move the group towards taking their own initiative for developing their knowledge.

Kaur (2015) used an online discussion forum for in-service TESOL teachers in Malaysia on their teaching of writing and also noted how they need to be facilitated by a teacher educator in order to stimulate their reflections and specifically assisted in relinquishing control (i.e., structure, overt guidance) to provide opportunity (i.e., freedom, space) for learners to write. Kaur (2015) observed that it is vitally important for the teacher educator on such an in-service TESOL course to provide the teachers with a space (or activity-centered learning) for reflection as they negotiate their perceptions of writing.

Bai (2014) also reported on the importance of a facilitator for stimulating reflection with in-service TESOL teachers in Hong Kong during post-observation conferences about the teaching of writing. Bai (2014) reported that when such discussions were aided by a facilitator, the teachers were encouraged to develop their own personal theories of teaching writing and to become more confident in their ability to teach writing. According to Bai (2014), the teachers were able to problematize their own practices by noting the problems in practice and then work out their own practical solutions with the aid of the facilitator's input. In such a reflective process the teachers said that the facilitator and the teachers acted as "mirrors" to help "see" each other's issues related to practice and, as a result, they were able to develop their own personal theory of teaching writing.

Some studies added the reflective element of action research and collaborative action research to that of feedback from peers and a facilitator to enhance reflections on practice and planning and report positive results of this combination, although the same issue of power relations that arose for pre-service teachers above was also an issue for some in-service TESOL teachers. For a general perspective, Wyatt (2011: 422), for example, noted that as a result of engaging in action research as part of their reflections on practice and planning, in-service TESOL teachers in Oman not only developed their research skills, but also were able to address important concerns that related to the contexts they worked in and how the context impacted their planning and instructional delivery. Cirocki, Tennekoon, and Pena Calvo (2014) also reported that generally when in-service TESOL teachers in Sri Lanka engage in reflections on their practice and planning with the aid of action research along with feedback, they not only see the value of reflective practice but now also have a voice that can replace the historical vacuum of their silence in the past. This is important, because as Cirocki, Tennekoon, and Pena Calvo (2014: 25) note, the teachers can now be "considered to be active agents that contribute immensely to the development of school curriculum, course and materials design as well as classroom-based research."

Banegas, Pavese, Velázquez, and Vélez (2013) encouraged collaborative reflection for in-service TESOL teachers in Argentina and discovered that it stimulated greater awareness of the impact of planning on practice and vice versa and this led to deeper reflection. Banegas et al. (2013) noted that although the TESOL teachers had individual and different motives for engaging in such reflection on their practice, interestingly they all developed at the same pace. As Banegas et al. (2013: 191) observed, "collaborative reflection stimulated individual reflection and vice versa." As they began then to develop as a team, Banegas et al. (2013: 193) observed that the teachers "felt more comfortable and flexible as regards topics, lesson planning and materials development." The result of such reflections impacted students' learning in a positive manner as they too felt that their motivation to learn increased and they perceived this had a beneficial impact on their language proficiency.

Dajani (2015: 133) reported that when in-service TESOL teachers in Ramallah were encouraged to reflect on their practice and lesson planning through action research along with feedback from peers and a facilitator, they could better detach themselves from their practice and "consider and develop their own solutions to problems." In such a collaborative manner and similar to what Banegas et al. (2013) discovered, but unlike the results of what was reported in Chan (2015), Dajani (2015) reported that the teachers became more autonomous, and helped them to be more accountable and responsible for their practices, not to mention their reported improvement and positive changes in their teaching practices. As Dajani (2015: 134) remarked, "they have developed reflective, analytical skills and have experienced the importance of being a life-long learner through using inquiry as an approach for the purpose of improving classroom instruction." This has also led to improvements in classroom interaction and students' engagement, similarly to what has been reported in Banegas et al. (2013) above.

Chan (2015) also examined the collaboration practices in a large-scale school-university capacity-building collaborative action research project in Hong Kong. In this case the in-service TESOL teachers chose their own research focus, and data collection methods. The teacher educators provided regular online support to help the in-service teachers implement two cycles of action research over a six-month period. The support provided by the teacher educators included helping the teachers to identify their research focus, co-planning the action research and assisting in the data collection process. In an interesting discovery and similar to what Engin (2015) reported for pre-service TESOL teachers in Turkey, Chan (2015) reported that the approach did not achieve success because of various power dynamics at play, some of which reflected institutional and societal practices (within the context of Hong Kong). As Chan (2015: 121) observed, "shared power and equity were not achieved in this project" and noted that it was the in-service TESOL teachers that resisted any equal status because they considered the facilitators as experts. Chan (2015) observed that throughout the reflective process the in-service teachers were more cooperative than collaborative as a result of their perceptions of these power differentials. This could also be the result of top-down institutionally imposed collaborative actions research and reflective practice rather than bottom-up reflective practice where individual teachers engage in their own reflections with or without a facilitator.

Reflective Questions

- How can in-service TESOL teachers engage in self-monitoring of their teaching practices and examine how these impact their theory and vice versa?
- Why would TESOL teachers with lots of teaching experience be reluctant to reflect on their practice?
- How can in-service TESOL teachers address the affective side of classroom observations?
- One study reported that the most frequent reactions from those in-service TESOL teachers averse to being observed were uneasiness, distrust, insecurity and anxiety about having an observer in class with them. Have you ever experienced any of these feelings associated with classroom observations? If so, how did you handle them? If not, how would you advise an in-service teacher to handle them?
- What are the advantages and disadvantages of peers reflecting together?
- Why would peers be reluctant to provide negative feedback?
- Do you think that peers need to be "trained" on how to provide feedback on theory and practice to other peers or other teachers within a group? If yes, how should they be trained?

- What are the advantages and disadvantages of groups of teachers coming together to reflect on their theory and practice?
- How can a group of teachers with different levels of teaching experience who come together to reflect on their theory and practice put aside their different personalities and backgrounds?
- In what ways could a facilitator stimulate reflection in a group?
- One study noted that a vacuum has been created by the silence of TESOL teachers because they have historically had no voice in matters concerning their practice. However, engaging in reflective practice with the aid of action research can be liberating for such teachers because they can now become active agents in the development of their practice. What is your understanding of this shift?
- One study noted that similarly to what was reported for pre-service teachers, the issue of power relations arose when in-service TESOL teachers were encouraged to engage in a large-scale school-university collaborative action research project with support provided by facilitators. However, the teachers resisted because of their perception that the facilitators were experts and as such the teachers did see themselves as equals when reflecting on their practice. What is your understanding of this issue of power differentials in this case?
- What is the difference between top-down reflective practice and bottom-up reflective practice for in-service TESOL teachers?

Conclusion

This chapter reviewed studies that encouraged pre-service and in-service TESOL teachers to reflect on their practice. Because not many studies focused primarily on practice without reference to other stages on the framework such as theory, and especially planning and lesson study, this combination (practice and theory) was also included in the chapter. It is interesting when encouraged to reflect on practice (and theory), both pre-service TESOL teachers and in-service TESOL teachers tended to be reluctant to enter into deep reflections unless they were prompted in some manner. For pre-service TESOL teachers it seems that some form of mentorship and guidance is necessary in order to stimulate teachers to move beyond descriptive reflections on practice, otherwise they will engage in self-blame because they focus mostly on their own classroom behaviors and less on their students' learning. However, the results of most studies suggest that whenever feedback was provided, the pre-service TESOL teachers seemed to make clearer connections between theory and practice. This seems important, too, for in-service TESOL teachers because if left alone to reflect or in pairs or groups, the studies reviewed noted that they may be reluctant at first to give (and receive) critical feedback for fear of offending others. For in-service TESOL teachers the important role of facilitator was highlighted in many studies as a form of intervention to help stimulate critical reflection on practice and theory. For both pre-service and in-service TESOL teachers it seems that a facilitator (teacher educator, supervisor, senior colleague or the like) can provide the teachers with a space for reflection as they negotiate their perceptions of their practice. The next chapter reviews studies related to the practices that encourage TESOL teachers to reflect beyond practice.

7

BEYOND PRACTICE

Introduction

In the previous chapter I reviewed the research about when TESOL teachers are encouraged to reflect on their practice and especially its combination with theory, but where practice was the main focus of the combination. In this chapter I proceed to review research that encourages TESOL teachers to reflect related to the final stage of the framework, namely reflecting beyond their practice and how it is combined with other stages of the framework for reflecting on practice.

When TESOL teachers are encouraged to reflect beyond practice, this is sometimes called *critical reflection* because it entails exploring and examining the moral, political and social issues that impact a teacher's practice both inside and outside the classroom. Thus such critical reflection takes on a sociocultural dimension that includes all aspects of a teacher's professional life outside the classroom and links practice more closely to the broader socio-political as well as affective issues that impact a teacher's classroom practice. Such a critical focus on reflections also includes teachers examining the moral aspect of practice and the moral values and judgments that impact practice. As noted above, teaching is heavily influenced by social forces and political trends, as there is the possibility of the presence of different types of discrimination inherent in different educational systems. In other words, no practice is without philosophy, principles, theory or ideology (hence the framework is inclusive of all five). Indeed, it can be said that every practice promotes some sort of ideology, so as I have written elsewhere it is always best for TESOL teachers to be aware of what is fueling their actual class-room practices ideologically (Farrell, 2015a). Consequently, reflections beyond practice can assist TESOL teachers in becoming more aware of the many political agendas and economic interests that can (and do) shape how we define language teaching and learning. They can become more aware of the impact of their lessons on society and the impact of society on their practice by consciously engaging in critical pedagogy or critical action research, an extension of action research in the previous level. This chapter outlines the research related to pre-service and in-service TESOL teachers' reflections beyond practice as its main focus along with its various other combinations with other aspects of the framework such as principles, theory and practice (combinations with philosophy was covered in Chapter 3).

Pre-service Teachers' Reflections Beyond Practice

When the focus of pre-service TESOL teachers' reflections was beyond practice and in combinations with principles, theory and practice, many of the reviewed studies noted that reflections were moved beyond a focus on teaching methodology and techniques to a more critical stance toward the profession as a whole with most studies reporting pre-service TESOL teachers experiencing a transformative reflective experience. Encouraging pre-service TESOL teachers in Iran to use journal writing to encourage reflection, Abednia (2012) for example, examined the ways critical TESOL teacher education contributes to TESOL teachers' overall development. As a result, Abednia (2012: 713) noted that the TESOL teachers adopted "a critical and transformative approach to their career on their own initiative." Abednia (2012) remarked that such a critical stance toward language teacher education moved the teachers from a position of conformity with the dominant ideology that was present in language teacher education to a more critical autonomous position about their profession as a whole. As Abednia (2012: 713) reported, during this critical approach to teacher education, the TESOL teachers became more aware of their old uncritical habits and attitudes and "more conscious of limitations imposed on them by authorities and institutions." In this manner, as a result of critical reflections, they also began to redefine their own positions, rights, and roles within the profession. As Abednia (2012: 712) observed, many of the teachers experienced a shift from thinking of "ELT as merely aimed at teaching ESL/EFL" to "going beyond language instruction and fulfilling educationally oriented promises such as helping people become critical thinkers and active citizens."

He and Prater (2014) also examined the written reflections of pre-service TESOL teachers in the US in order to see how such a prompt can promote critical reflection in a teacher education course. The teacher educators incorporated a community-based service learning project (that integrated classroom instruction with community service activities) into a graduate-level ESL teacher preparation course where the pre-service teachers would work one-on-one with English language learners. The idea was that such a community-based service learning approach would enable the pre-service teachers to develop not only self-esteem and self-efficacy, but also as He and Prater (2014: 33) noted, "positive views of diverse others, ethic of caring, and other cultural competencies ... in a situated, authentic context." Similarly to what Abednia (2012) noted above, He and Prater (2014) also noted that not all the teachers were able to move towards a critical reflective stance. In fact, most of the participants were descriptive in their reflections and very few were critical (only 12 percent of the teachers). As a result, He and Prater (2014: 43) suggested that the teachers may require some scaffolding to help them make such a shift and note that it is "critical for teacher educators to make the connections between the project and reflection explicit, and intentionally teach the reflective skills to better prepare teachers for the community-based service learning projects." Thus, incorporating some kind of service learning into language teacher education programs can help prompt pre-service TESOL teachers to reflect beyond their classroom practices.

Birbirso (2012) also examined what can be done to facilitate effective critical reflection for pre-service TESOL teachers in teacher education programs in Ethiopia. Birbirso (2012) noted that the activities and assessment instruments that pre-service TESOL teachers were presented with in their practicum training may actually be constraining their shift towards critical reflection because they were very structured, performance-oriented observation checklists that were underpinned by a pre-defined objectives approach. As Birbirso (2012: 862) pointed out, this system of reflection is prescribed by teacher educators in order to evaluate "their teaching on a five-point Likert scale, i.e. from poor grade to the best grade of excellent" and as a result, "one of the core factors for student teachers' difficulty is a lack of bottom-up reflective tools." Birbirso (2012) reported that the pre-service TESOL teachers tended to conceal information about themselves and others in the early stages of reflection and not reveal what they were really thinking about in terms of taking a critical stance on practice. Consequently, and similar to the findings of He and Prater (2014) above, Birbirso (2012: 867) maintained that teacher educators should not always be evaluating but rather should provide some scaffolding for their pre-service TESOL teachers in the form of "generative reflection tools, rather than work towards sheer assessment of student teachers on pre-set competency checklists at a faculty level." Birbirso (2012) observed that such action strategies as reflective journaling and reflective discussions on those journal entries can enhance pre-service TESOL teachers' reflective learning. As a result of their journal writing, Birbirso (2012: 865) observed that the teachers were not only able to reflect on their own assumptions, beliefs, and theories and how they could use this information to improve their practice, but they could also make the shift beyond practice and take a more critical stance on "wider school practices and issues and how they relate to classroom behaviors, actions and interactions."

More specifically Hernandez (2015) was interested in encouraging pre-service TESOL teachers in Columbia to critically reflect on one of their teacher education courses, second language acquisition (SLA), to see if the pre-service teachers can gain a better understanding of how this course can not only impact their teaching practices but also their lives as TESOL teachers within the profession. Using regular reflective journal entries and a written report on an observed class where SLA was the focus of practice, Hernandez (2015) reported that such reflective prompts enabled the pre-service teachers to consider their students' learning as related to SLA instruction and how they as practitioners focused on their future work as English language teachers in the context of Columbia. Hernandez (2015) noted that the results suggest that the pre-service teachers were able to become more critically reflective on the role of SLA instruction both inside and outside the classroom and provided valuable information about the impact of course materials and class activities to raise their awareness of the importance of SLA on their theory of teaching. As Hernandez (2015: 147) pointed out, the results "may be indicative of an emerging teaching and learning theory of participants and document a possible change in perceptions as a result of reflection and course activities such as lesson observation and journal writing." In addition, Hernandez (2015) observed that taking a more expansive and critical stance on their role as future English language teachers, helped them realize that they could take on the role as social agents to promote changes that impact their learners' lives. As Hernandez (2015: 147) pointed out, "The use of reflective writings allowed documentation of participants' awareness of their role to bring about change in students' lives, thus confirming that personal practical knowledge has a moral and emotional dimension as well."

Similar to the findings of Hernandez (2015) of raising awareness of moral, emotional and social dimensions of practice, Deng and Yuen (2011), using blogs to promote such critical reflection, also reported increased awareness of enhancing the socio-emotional dimension of a learning community of pre-service TESOL teachers in Hong Kong. Deng and Yuen (2011) noted that the blogs enabled the pre-service TESOL teachers to make a shift in their reflections from an initial purely cognitive focus to a later more emotional dimension where the teachers were able to note the impact of practice on their personal lives; as Deng and Yuen (2011) noted, this emotional dimension of reflection is often downplayed in teacher education programs but it is very important for pre-service teachers who are on a practicum. As Deng and Yuen (2011) observed, pre-service TESOL teachers are very vulnerable while on teaching practice because they must struggle to cope with many different dilemmas and insecurities while they are forming their roles and lives as English language teachers. Thus, Deng and Yuen (2011) suggest that the pre-service TESOL teachers be provided with a means of releasing and reflecting on their emotions during this very important stage in their formation as teachers. Deng and Yuen (2011: 449) continue, "Hence a risk-free channel through which one could vent became invaluable in order to cope with one's emotions, wrestle with dilemmas, and come to better terms with classroom reality." The use of blogs, according to Deng and Yuen (2011), not only helped the teachers to express and reflect on their emotions but were also socially oriented as they noted they were not written just for each pre-service TESOL teacher, but also for the reflection and dialogue of others.

Reflective Questions

- One study reported that TESOL teacher education moved the teachers from a position of conformity with the dominant ideology present in language teacher education to a more critical autonomous position about their profession as a whole. Do you agree that pre-service TESOL teachers should be encouraged to critically reflect on the profession in such a manner? If yes, why? If no, why not?
- Although some TESOL teacher education programs may encourage pre-service TESOL teachers to take a critically reflective stance on their practice, some studies noted that not all the teachers were able to make such a move towards a critical reflective stance. Why do you think this is so?
- One study suggested that one of the core factors for student teachers' difficulty in making a shift from descriptive to critical reflection is a lack of bottom-up reflective tools. What is your understanding of this?
- Some studies suggest that some scaffolding should be incorporated in TESOL teacher education programs if they want their pre-service teachers to become more critically reflective. What kind of scaffolding would be appropriate?
- Some studies note the importance of the emotional dimension in developing critical reflection but note that this is somewhat overlooked in many TESOL teacher education programs because they only focus on the cognitive aspect of practice. What is your understanding of emotions connected to critical reflection? Why do you think it is often overlooked?
- How can TESOL teacher educators encourage pre-service teachers to release and reflect on the emotional dimension of practice and what means can they provide to help them do this?
- Do you think that pre-service TESOL teachers should be encouraged to take on the role as social agents to promote changes that impact their learners' lives? If yes, why and how? If no, why not?

In-service Teachers' Reflections Beyond Practice

When in-service TESOL teachers were encouraged to reflect beyond practice in combination with philosophy, principles, theory and practice, most of the studies reported that the teachers reflected well beyond their classroom teaching practices on such issues as the textbooks they are given to teach, the syllabus and curriculum they are given and their working conditions, especially what they are expected to do by the administration rather than what they think their professional roles are.

Sangani and Stelma (2012) for example, explored the reflections of an in-service TESOL teacher development group in Iran as they reflected on their philosophy, beliefs, theory, and practice, and beyond practice. Sangani and Stelma (2012) reported that the in-service TESOL teachers focused their reflections on such issues as their pedagogical and content knowledge, the textbooks and the curriculum they had to follow as well as the official syllabus they had to use, and their actual working conditions. Sangani and Stelma (2012) noted that as a result of their discussions and critical reflections, the in-service TESOL teachers were able to identify the various challenges they faced and how they present different ways of understanding such challenges as well as formulate plans of action. However, Sangani and Stelma (2012) noted that although the TESOL teachers worked collaboratively to raise their awareness of various aspects of practice and policy, they did not act on their stated plans. As Sangani and Stelma (2012: 127) observed, "There were few references to actions actually taken" and as a result they noted that, "the outcomes of reflection may need time to materialize." One reason the authors gave for this was the possibility of the contextual constraints. That said, Sangani and Stelma (2012) remarked that together and over time they developed a heightened sense of professional agency.

Farrell (2011b) also examined the discussions of experienced in-service TESOL teachers in a teacher development group as they reflected on their professional role identity as ESL teachers in Canada. Farrell (2011b) reported 16 main professional role identities that emerged from the group discussions and these were further placed into three main clusters: Teacher as Manager, Teacher as "Acculturator" and Teacher as Professional. Teacher as manager, which had seven sub-identities, was identified as a role where the teacher is the person attempting to manage what happens within the classroom. Among the more frequently mentioned sub-identities within the teacher as manager cluster were teacher as vendor, teacher as entertainer, teacher as communication controller, teacher as juggler, teacher as motivator, teacher as presenter, and, teacher as arbitrator. Teacher as "acculturator," a term coined for this study, is used to identify a role where the teacher is seen as one who engages in activities outside the classroom and who helps students become accustomed to the local culture. The most frequently occurring sub-identities in this cluster were those of teacher as "socializer" and teacher as social worker. The teacher as professional role was identified where the teacher is seen as one who is dedicated to her work, and takes it very seriously. The most frequently occurring sub-identities in this cluster were teacher as collaborator, and teacher as learner. Farrell (2011b) noted that critical reflection in group discussions on teacher roles both inside and outside the classroom not only generates awareness of these roles, but also how they have been shaped over time and by whom. Unlike Sangani and Stelma (2012), Farrell (2011b) observed that critical reflections in the group allowed the teachers to take action on the need for more balance in who was "directing" these roles within their context, as they renegotiated many throughout the period of reflection.

In what could be viewed as a follow-up to the above study, Farrell (2015b) reported on teachers' perceptions of teacher–student relationships and how the nature of these relationships affects interactions between teachers and students both inside and outside the classroom. Farrell (2015b) has pointed out that for ESL teachers, the relational and emotional investment involved in teaching includes constant monitoring of and listening to how their students are feeling, and evaluating if they need assistance with their learning. Farrell (2015b) examined how they talked about these experiences with others in a teacher reflection group as a means of understanding how this knowledge influences what happens in the context of their work. Farrell (2015b) reported that the teachers noted that while realizing these relationships, they encountered a number of dilemmas, such as whether to entertain or not to entertain, and issues surrounding the degree of reciprocity in teacher–student relationships. Another important reflection by the teachers was the issue of boundary-setting or how the teachers set boundaries to help them limit their emotional involvement and exhaustion whilst maintaining positive teacher–student relationships. Although ESL teachers have invested heavily in building personal relationships with their ESL students both inside and outside the classroom, such relationship building according to Farrell (2015b) was at times rewarding but also exhausting. As Farrell (2015b: 33) remarked, the teachers noted that "it may be necessary to create some boundaries between teachers and students so that teachers can consider and maintain their own well-being." Thus Farrell (2015b) concludes that it is important for ESL teachers to articulate and critically reflect on these issues because they have important implications for the type and quality of teacher–student interactions both inside and outside the classroom.

Feng-ming Chi (2010) examined the reflections of in-service TESOL teachers in Taiwan and specifically how writing can stimulate critical reflections on their practice. Feng-ming Chi (2010) explored the in-service TESOL teachers' critical reflections on their philosophy, principles, theory and how these impact their actual classroom practices and beyond classroom practice. Feng-ming Chi's (2010) results concur with many of the studies reported on above for pre-service TESOL teachers, in that the act of reflective writing helped the in-service TESOL teachers reflect on more critical issues related to their overall work in their context and especially the impact of social issues on their role as TESOL teachers. They noted that such critical reflections not only helped the in-service TESOL teachers gain more awareness of these important issues but their learners also benefited from such increased awareness. As Feng-ming Chi (2010: 180) observed, the in-service TESOL teachers critically reflected on "deeper issues beyond practice, such as social issues, inequitable relationships and generated roles," thus enhancing "their critical thinking as both teachers and learners." Feng-ming Chi (2010) discovered that the in-service teachers first focused on their teaching methods before they moved onto more of a questioning mode of critical reflection in their later entries. This shift to a more critical stance came after the teachers became more comfortable asking themselves questions about their underlying assumptions about practice and beyond the classroom. As Feng-ming Chi (2010: 180) observed, reflective writing stimulated their reflections on their beliefs and practices. In fact, Feng-ming Chi (2010) remarked that this reflection could have possibly led to changes in their beliefs and practices as they began to redefine their beliefs and practices.

In this case reflection functioned as a recursive process in which the in-service TESOL teachers built upon each level into a deeper level of engagement; Feng-ming Chi (2010: 176) explained: "reflection kept occurring at deeper levels, building upon each discursive engagement toward more personal awareness of the relevant social issues, inequitable relationships and generated roles." Feng-ming Chi (2010) surmised that such a recursive type of critical reflection can enhance critical thinking for in-service TESOL teachers because it provides a means of articulating their philosophy, principles, theories, practices and beyond practice. It should also be pointed out that Feng-ming Chi (2010: 180) reported that most of the teachers reported that they were "enthusiastic and took pleasure in reflecting," whereas some reported "their discomfort with reflection via journal writing as a regular assignment." This was because for some reflection brought up some unpleasant experiences and they did not know how to deal with their contradictory or fragmented thoughts, feelings and reflections. In addition when asked to read their peers' journals, although they gained some new awareness about teaching possibilities, they also stated that they did not want to respond to these for fear of causing any problems or unnecessary tensions. In fact, as Feng-ming Chi (2010: 181) observed, "such feelings inhibited them from engaging in collaborative reflective inquiry, which most wanted to avoid unless they were 'forced to do so.'"

In a similar mode of encouraging reflection through writing, Farrell (2013b) explored how journal writing facilitated critical reflection for one experienced ESL college teacher in Canada who reflected on her philosophy, principles, theory, practice and beyond practice. Comparable to what Feng-ming Chi (2010) reported above, the TESOL teacher initially focused her reflections on her teaching effectiveness and later focused more on issues outside her classroom and beyond her practice. As Farrell (2013b: 470) noted, as a result of reflecting critically on her practice, the experienced TESOL teacher began to slowly "unpack any emotional baggage be it personal or professional and get beyond it." Such a mode of reflection enabled the teacher to enhance her personal and professional growth and development as it allowed her to not only identify issues important to her, but also to move beyond them. According to Farrell (2013b), such heightened awareness resulted in a change of her perception of self as an ESL professional as she gained more confidence inside and outside the classroom. Farrell (2013b: 470) remarked that the teacher in this case study stated that writing "forced me to slow down, observe and reflect," and although she was initially hesitant, apprehensive and skeptical about the writing process, she said that she "came to enjoy it."

In order to help teachers make changes in their lives as a result of their reflections, Ito (2012) has suggested that perhaps that they may need an "expansive visibilization" (EV) to enhance the critical reflection process because even if teachers recognize some problems in their practice, they may be resistant to making changes to their practice. Ito (2012), working in Japan, pointed out that EV in the form of diagrams like concept maps can help make work visible and more understandable and may stimulate critical reflection, especially in the initial stages of such reflections. Thus Ito (2012) looked at the critical reflections of two in-service TESOL teachers in Japan who used EV as a prompt and stimulus to aid their reflections and discovered that although both used the diagram, and both participants were able to elaborate on their reflections about their practice, their reflections varied substantially. According to Ito (2012), for the teacher who said he benefited from the use of EV, or the visible use of concept maps, such a stimulus seemed to give him a clearer perspective of his previously distorted image of teaching and helped him generate his own solutions to practice and beyond practice. As Ito (2012: 88) remarked, "through the process of EV, his reflections became more detailed and extended in scope to historical, cultural, and societal causes of contradictions." For the other teacher however, who did not seem to benefit from the use of EV, Ito (2012) reported that it could be that the facilitator did not actively support him in his inquiry. As Ito (2012: 89) observed, "Without this active support from the collaborator, EV might not differ a great deal from traditional action research, which operates without the triangular diagram." Thus when in-service TESOL teachers are encouraged to critically reflect beyond practice with the use of "expansive visibilization" methods, it seems that some scaffolding by a facilitator may be necessary in order to support such critical reflection.

Reflective Questions

- One study reported that although the in-service TESOL teachers were able to critically reflect on aspects of their practice such as a mandated curriculum and syllabus as well as mandated textbooks and the challenges they faced in their work, they did not manage to take any action or make any actual changes even though they were not happy. Why do you think this is the case?
- The study noted in the previous question suggested that critical reflection may take time. What is your understanding of this?
- In a different context a different study of in-service TESOL teachers reported that they were able to make changes as a result of their critical reflections. What is the role of context in such critical reflections?
- This study identified different professional roles as a result of the in-service TESOL teachers' reflections. What is your understanding of the following roles: "teacher as manager"; "teacher as vendor"; "teacher as entertainer"; "teacher as juggler"; "teacher as motivator"; "teacher as presenter"; "teacher as arbitrator"; "teacher as "acculturator"; "teacher as socializer"; "teacher as social worker"; "teacher as professional"; "teacher as collaborator"; "teacher as learner"; "teacher as knowledgeable"?
- The emotional investment involved in teaching TESOL according to one study includes constant monitoring of and listening to how students are feeling, and evaluating if they need assistance with their learning and as a

result TESOL teachers can burn out easily. However, this aspect of a TESOL teacher's life is not really recognized or appreciated by administrators or academics. What is your understanding of this?

- The in-service TESOL teachers in the above study said that they should set boundaries to help them limit their emotional involvement and exhaustion whilst maintaining positive teacher–student relationships. Do you agree or disagree? Explain your answer.
- One study suggests that when in-service TESOL teachers critically reflect on their practice, they not only gain more awareness of these important issues but their learners also benefited from such increased awareness. What is your understanding of this?
- Sometimes reflecting critically on all aspects of a TESOL teacher's work can bring up some unpleasant experiences and contradictory or fragmented thoughts and feelings. How can a teacher deal with these unpleasant experiences?
- One study suggested that "expansive visibilization" (EV) can enhance the critical reflective process of in-service TESOL teachers by extending the scope of reflections beyond the classroom to historical, cultural, and societal causes of contradictions. How can the use of EV such as concept mapping help in-service TESOL teachers critically reflect on their practice?

Conclusion

This chapter reviewed studies that encouraged pre-service and in-service TESOL teachers to reflect beyond practice. Because not many studies focused primarily on reflections beyond practice without reference to other stages, the studies reported here include combinations of philosophy, principles, theory and practice with beyond practice reflections. When pre-service TESOL teachers were encouraged to reflect beyond practice, many of the reviewed studies reviewed reported that the pre-service teachers were able to take a more critically reflective position towards their future profession and as a result found the process transformative. However, some studies also noted that pre-service TESOL teachers found it difficult at times to move beyond descriptive reflection and take a deeper critical stance without some help from a supervisor and/or facilitator, especially when considering the emotional dimension of such reflections. Most in-service TESOL teachers, when encouraged to reflect beyond practice, reported positive results when reflecting on mandated curriculum, working conditions and professional roles; however, context seems to be an important consideration when the teachers want to make actual changes as a result of such critical reflections. The next chapter reviews and appraises the reflective instruments or tools most commonly used in the studies that were reviewed.

8

REFLECTIVE PRACTICE INSTRUMENTS

Introduction

The studies reviewed so far in this book all used different reflective instruments or tools to assist and facilitate the TESOL teachers with their reflections. The research indicates that TESOL teachers have a range of viable reflective instruments/tools at their disposal that included 37 instruments in all. This chapter examines the kind of reflective practice instruments that both pre-service and in-service TESOL teachers used to facilitate the process of engaging in reflective practice. Given that there were so many different instruments used, and in the interests of space, the chapter will focus its appraisal on the most frequently used reflective instruments in all 138 studies under review.

Reflective Instruments

In terms of the main reflective practice instruments or tools used (it should be noted that there was some overlap that was difficult to separate) especially regarding their rate of use to encourage and facilitate reflection in the studies that were reviewed, discussion (including teacher discussion groups and post-observation conferences) was the most frequently used in this body of research, followed by writing and this was closely followed by classroom observations (self, peer, etc. with or without video/audio), and then by a much lesser frequency, action research. After these, the other less popular reflective instruments include narrative study and then lesson study but these are used infrequently. Instruments used in three or fewer instances included: cases, portfolios, team teaching, peer coaching, and critical friend/incident transcript reflections. The section that follows provides some more details about the major reflective tools, discussion, writing, classroom observations, action research and to a lesser extent, narrative study, that appear in the order and frequency of use outlined in the 138 studies reviewed in this book.

Discussion

The most frequently used reflective practice instrument used in many of the studies reviewed was some kind of discussion (again with some overlap with other instruments but with discussion as the dominant instrument), with the most popular type centered around discussions in a teacher reflection group (sometimes called teacher development group or teacher study group) where the participants all noted that they were building a community of practice, because engagement in group discussions allowed the TESOL teachers (either pre-service or in-service) to voice their ideas about various issues related to their practice, which in turn helped them feel a sense of community while they were engaged in their teacher group discussions. Some of these discussions were face-to-face and included post-observation conference discussions that were important in encouraging reflection, while others were online in nature. I present an analysis of each of the different types of discussions in terms of their frequency of use with the most frequently used, group discussion, first.

An example of face-to-face type teacher group discussions was in Ahmadi, Samad, and Noordin's (2013) study, which examined how pre-service TESOL teachers' engagement through discourse socialization practices in their graduate TEFL program influences their professional identity development. The courses focused mostly on oral discourse practices including small group discussions, and less attention was paid to written discourse practices. The pre-service TESOL teachers gave oral presentations, engaged in whole-class discussions after oral presentations, did task-based small group discussions and wrote reflection papers on the assigned reading materials. Ahmadi, Samad, and Noordin (2013: 1745) reported that encouraging pre-service TESOL teachers to reflect in group discussions "had a very significant influence on the identity construction of the participants. The participants assumed more professional identity over time due to engagement in new discourse and practices." In particular, they noted that reflecting in such group discussions helped the pre-service TESOL teachers to reconsider their understanding of their professional identity and its probable shift, because it will continue to evolve over time. As Ahmadi, Samad, and Noordin (2013: 1765) remarked, encouraging these TESOL teachers to engage in group discussions allowed them to realize that a TESOL "teacher's identity is a continuous process of being informed, formed, and reformed which develops over time mostly through having interactions with other members of their discourse community and also through reflection over teaching practices."

Likewise, Farrell (2014a) noted the positive impact of teacher group discussions, this time for three female experienced TESOL teachers who had conveyed before the group formation that they felt they had "plateaued professionally" and thus were in need of some kind of renewal. They approached the author to help facilitate their reflections through regular group discussions. Farrell (2014a: 515) reported that reflecting in these group discussions over a two-year period with weekly group meetings during the academic terms of the first year and follow-up meetings during the second year, helped the teachers "break feelings of isolation and overcome feelings of plateauing." Farrell (2014a: 515) remarked that these experienced TESOL teachers reported that the weekly face-to-face group discussions helped them validate "each other's experiences, gave support, sympathy, and encouragement, held up similar experiences for comparison, and compared our different teaching styles," as they regained their enthusiasm for their work. Because they were encouraged to reflect in such group discussions, Farrell (2014a: 516) observed that they were able to articulate their perceptions about their practice and as a result "sort out important issues related to their learners and their colleagues and they became less skeptical about their career as [TESOL] teachers once they had talked through many of the issues."

Hung and Yeh (2013) also reported positive outcomes for a teacher reflection group (five TESOL teachers and one group facilitator) for professional development. Hung and Yeh (2013) observed that when the TESOL teachers were encouraged to reflect during nine bi-weekly group meetings in an 18-week period in group interactive discussions they began to share their practical knowledge as well as co-design several teaching activities and at the same time self-appraise their classroom teaching. These were similar topics as those reported in the Farrell (2014a) study above. Hung and Yeh (2013) also noted the importance of facilitation in group discussions even for experienced TESOL teachers; Hung and Yeh (2013: 163) continue:

> Even the teachers with many years of teaching experience still needed stimulus and support to promote their continuous learning. With facilitation for developing their practical knowledge in collaborative learning activities, they could easily extend their professional knowledge, take initiative in their own implementation, and evolve their own ongoing inquiry.

In a more recent study of attempts to cultivate a TESOL community of practice (CoP) for sustainable professional development, Mak and Pun (2015) reported on a series of planned efforts in cultivating a group of 18 TESOL teachers into such a CoP in Hong Kong over a period of ten months. Such planned efforts included the teachers attending a summer institute as a focal point of the project that provided an opportunity for systematically observing how teachers learned from each other and as a group through a series of teacher demonstrations, and reading-response group meetings. Mak and Pun (2015: 18) noted that the group went through different stages of development, such as "forging a group identity in the midst of tensions arising out of different personalities and/or backgrounds, building common goals, resolving cognitive and psychological dissonances for professional learning and development, as well as assuming communal responsibility for sustainable professional development." They also observed that for such teacher groups to survive, it is up to individuals to be committed, honest, self-aware and sensitive so that they can "develop their expertise-in-self in the process" (Mak & Pun, 2015: 19). In terms of sustainability, however, they wonder what will happen to this group once they return to work and face different daily demands that may not allow time for such future commitment to the continuation of the group.

In a different type of group discussion setting, Waring (2013) has pointed out the importance of post-observation discussions and in particular, issues of reflective practices in post-observation conferences. Waring (2013) has noted that suggestions for promoting reflection in such post-observation discussions have included talking less and being less directive, withholding value judgments or unsolicited feedback, asking mediational questions such as "how do you think the lesson went?" and making open-ended statements about some aspects of teaching. Indeed, the importance of post-observation discussions as a means of encouraging TESOL teachers (both pre-service and in-service) has received a lot of attention in the studies reviewed in this book. For example, the importance of discussions during post-observation conferences to encourage reflection for pre-service teachers was reported on by Gan (2014), who noted their positive effects for NNEST pre-service teachers. In particular, Gan (2014: 133) observed that these post-observation discussions between the "supporting teacher and the student teacher proved to be very helpful particularly to those student teachers who were experiencing difficulties in delivering lesson contents and engaging students in learning activities." In addition, such discussions, Gan (2014) pointed out, can help iron out any misunderstandings and dissatisfaction that can occur between pre-service TESOL teachers and their supervisors.

In an interesting report on collaborative dialogue between pre-service TESOL teachers and supervisors in post-observation sessions supported by video recordings, Kaneko-Marques (2015) reported positive effects such as the pre-service TESOL teachers being better able to analyze their practice, and even (re)construct it to favor their students' language learning process rather than their own needs as teachers. As Kaneko-Marques (2015: 25) observed, "During the reflective and collaborative post-observation sessions, the student teachers established connections with theoretical course content, previous learning and teaching experiences, and their personal knowledge when analyzing their pedagogical actions in videotaped lessons." Kaneko-Marques (2015) concluded that such collaborative discussions between facilitators, supervisors and learner teachers can encourage the teachers to identify and understand the complexities of language learning, instead of formulating technical and universal solutions that might not cater to the specific needs of different educational contexts.

Farr and Riordan (2012) outlined the positive results in what they called "post-observation trainer trainee interactions" (POTTI) and teacher group discussions along with blogs and diaries, and online chats to encourage pre-service TESOL teachers to reflect. Farr and Riordan (2012) observed that based on all 14 one-to-one feedback discussion sessions from the post-observation trainer trainee interactions or POTTI, total tutor talk accounted for 63 percent and learner teacher talk for nearly 37 percent, which they noted was in line with other findings in related research. Although they noted that the tutor can be seen to speak almost twice as much as the learner teachers, they suggest we should look at this holistically and that the results are very encouraging, as they actually point to the highly interactive nature of such post-observation discussions. As Farr and Riordan (2012: 135) point out: The POTTI data "contains 82,000 words, 5776 turns, giving 70.45 turns per 1000 words – almost three times in excess of the 25 suggested by *Csomay* as an indicator of high interactivity." In addition, they note that the POTTI contains the least amount of positive nouns but that this is to be expected as they are novice teachers, "and the context is one of critical reflection, they may be focusing more on their negative teaching practice experiences and areas in need of improvement the next time round" (Farr & Riordan, 2012: 138).

The importance of discussions during post-observation conferences to encourage reflection for in-service TESOL teachers was reported on by Bai (2014) on helping Hong Kong in-service primary school TESOL teachers improve on their writing instruction through a school-based professional development program. Different than most other studies on the importance of these discussions however, is that it reported on how the facilitator can encourage the TESOL teachers to reflect on their own after the official process/project has finished.

The process consisted of first, the facilitator holding a meeting and discussing the recommended teaching principles, e.g. process writing. The teachers shared their views on the principles and explained how they might apply them in their teaching. Then, the two teachers in each school observed each other teaching in their writing lessons. The teachers could try out new methods or use methods they had used before. Third, in the post-teaching conferencing session, the facilitator asked the two teachers to recall their teaching process and to provide suggestions and comments to each other with reference to the recommended teaching principles. At the same time, the researcher offered his feedback. As a result of being encouraged to discuss their reflections in the post-observation conference, Bai (2014) noted that the two teachers reflected on and pro-blematized their own practices; as Bai (2014: 435) observed: "They saw their own problems in teaching and then worked out practical solutions with the research-er's help." As they gained more experience reflecting on their practices, Bai (2014: 436) reported that the teachers became more confident as they had developed a personal theory of teaching how to write because they noted that their "colleagues could work well as their 'mirrors' to see each other's problems in teaching as they were familiar with their students and each other's situations." Bai (2014) suggested that other teachers can use these similar three steps for reflecting on their practice, and especially noted the importance of the post-observation conferences, but these can also be eliminated when the teachers become familiar with the reflection process. As Bai (2014: 435) concluded: The facilitator's role "can be minimized or removed when school teachers are more familiar with the rationale and teaching principles."

In terms of online discussions, Guerrero Nieto and Meadows (2015: 14), for example, encouraged TESOL teachers, both pre-service and in-service, to reflect in online discussions and were particularly interested in how "graduate TESOL students' dialogues provide them with spaces to activate critical awareness of their global professional identity." According to Guerrero Nieto and Meadows (2015: 14), the graduate TESOL teachers were presented with three critical readings and asked them to form dialogue exchanges around their reactions to these readings. Then, after each reading, students from one group would post messages to what they called the "Schoology Wall" (Guerrero Nieto & Meadows, 2015: 15). After that, students in the counterpart group would put comments following each post, and a conversation chain would develop as commenters responded back and forth to the posts. As a result of these online discussions, Guerrero Nieto and Meadows (2015) noted that several themes emerged, such as the role of ELT, institutional constraints, whose culture to teach, linguistic diversity in language teaching, as well as differences in how the two groups developed those themes. They concluded that the more experienced TESOL teachers offered a narrative of empowerment in which most of their discourse was about challenging conventional boundaries in ELT. In contrast, the novice teachers put together a narrative of induction, whose discourse originated from their experience as learners; as Guerrero Nieto and Meadows (2015: 25) remarked: "the [expert] participants had had a long-term effect on how the [novice] participants envisioned their future teaching practices."

Kabilan, Adlina, and Embi (2011) also noted the positive impact of such online collaborative discussions, not only in terms of helping educators to evaluate learner teachers but also as a means of professional development for TESOL teachers, as the discussions resulted in having a positive impact on their classroom practices. As Kabilan, Adlina, and Embi (2011: 112) observed, "For many of the teachers, it molded and streamlined their thoughts on future classroom practices that would be meaningful and effective."

In an interesting study on the use of keypals (similar to pen pals but on email) Wach (2015) wondered how pre-service TESOL teachers would benefit from collaborating online with keypals from another country and what evidence of reflections would emerge from their interactions. Wach (2015) observed that many of the email reflections of the pre-service TESOL teachers were mostly technical in nature and not very deep as they focused primarily on descriptions of behavior. However, Wach (2015) did note that some pre-service teachers made attempts at deeper, more critical reflections by linking previous experiences to their present situation, and by making references to what their partner wrote and evaluating it critically. Wach (2015: 41) reported that the keypals created a "form of support community, and the interactions were evaluated as both informative and enjoyable and had a positive affective effect on them personally."

Riordan and Murray (2010; 2012) examined the interactional patterns within pre-service TESOL teacher and peer mentor discussions using forums, blogs and chats as well as face-to-face discussions. Riordan and Murray (2010: 194) reported positively about the interactivity of online communication because they said it had the "potential to aid professional development, by allowing for reflection, support, and collaborative problem-solving." They maintained that online communications were different from spoken discourse especially in terms of interactivity, turn length and informality. As Riordan and Murray (2010: 194) observed, discussion forums were similar to spoken discourse in terms of interactivity, "but carry a greater resemblance towards the written mode, possibly as a result of the time allowed to ponder over the discourse, thus allowing editing and reformulating of ideas." Riordan and Murray (2012) also noted that blogs and chats were highly interactive, social, and emotional and online discussion forums more cognitive but reflection is possible within both modes.

Chik and Breidbach (2011) and Chick (2015) noted how dialogic interaction and exploratory talk during post-teaching practice discussions can be beneficial to pre-service second language teacher education. Chik and Breidbach (2011) in particular used a combination of (wiki) discussion forum, social media, Facebook, and videoconferencing among other modes of reflection and observed that the combined online mode helped facilitate the learner teachers' identity development. Chick (2015) was also interested in further developing this approach to help promote long-term reflective practice and how enquiry-based talk raises awareness of the complexity involved in developing pedagogic expertise. Thus, Chick (2015) suggested that each practicum class be followed by a reflective group discussion by the learner teachers, chaired by the researcher/teacher educator who asked exploratory questions to prompt reflection. Chick (2015) observed that such exploratory talk opened the discussions for the learner teachers to reflect on their idea of a successful lesson. As Chick (2015: 304) remarked, such reflective conversations gave the learner teachers "opportunities to draw on and consider the theoretical aspects of their pre-service education and thus aid the reframing of their emergent understandings of language teaching."

So it seems that there may still be conflicting views about whether face-to-face or online discussions may be more reflective; both foster sharing and collaboration and lead to reflection but we still do not know what level this reflection is at. For some TESOL teachers, reflecting in blogs was more social than critically reflective and so dialoging with others may have taken precedence over taking a critical reflective stance on their practice or challenging others to reflect critically on their practice (Deng & Yuen, 2011). As Deng and Yuen (2011: 449) observed, "Blogging was not just about keeping account of personal events, but reaching out and updating others on what had happened; it was not just about releasing emotional tension, but seeking social connections and support as well."

In a more recent study Farr and Riordan (2015: 18) discovered that blogs are preferred mostly because "blogs, in particular, foster narration, RP, and the expression of identities." Future research may be able to shed more light on this interesting and important issue of online reflective tools and which tools help promote and foster more critical reflection.

Reflective Questions

- Why do you think that discussions as a means of encouraging TESOL teachers to reflect were the most popular mode or instrument of reflection?
- What is your understanding of the differences between face-to-face discussions, post-observation conferences/discussions and online discussions?
- Which type of discussion will lead to deep reflections and why?
- Why do you think that face-to-face teacher group discussions can "break feelings of isolation and overcome feelings of plateauing," as the results of one study noted?
- One study of face-to-face teacher group discussions suggested that even teachers with many years of teaching experience still needed stimulus and support to promote their continuous learning. Why do you think that such groups will need to be stimulated to reflect on their practice?
- Another study reported on the different stages the group went through, such as forging a group identity, building common goals, resolving cognitive and psychological dissonances for professional learning and development, and assuming communal responsibility for development. What is your understanding of these different stages and why do you think such groups will go through these different stages?
- Why do you think that post-observation discussions/conferences are important for fostering and encouraging reflection?
- Have you ever used keypals to foster reflection? Why do you think the study reported that the learner teachers were not very reflective with such a reflective instrument?
- How do you think online modes of reflective discussions could be different from regular spoken discourse?
- Why do you think that when blogging, some TESOL teachers did not always dialogue reflectively, as they did not challenge each other's opinions or give different ideas or push understandings, and the majority of the comments were of a social nature?
- Why do you think that there are conflicting views about which mode of reflection is deeper, face-to-face or online discussions? Which do you prefer and why?

Writing

Writing was the second most frequently used reflective practice instrument to encourage TESOL teachers (both pre-service and in-service) to engage in reflective practice. I present an analysis of the different types of writing used to foster reflection by pre-service TESOL teachers first and this is followed by in-service TESOL teachers' use of writing.

Golombek and Doran (2014) encouraged pre-service TESOL teachers to write a journal each week and then email it to the teacher educator. The teacher educator provided the topic for the first journal, written before actual teaching practice began, in order to capture what the pre-service TESOL teachers considered their expectations of the internship was, and their strengths and concerns as they embarked on their teaching experience. In subsequent journals, the pre-service TESOL teachers wrote descriptions of what they were doing in their classes, and their reactions to their teaching. The teacher educator responded to all journal entries directly in the documents, and the teacher educator's comments in the results section can be identified by being in italics. Golombek and Doran (2014: 110) then reported on the nature of the interns' journal reflections as containing mostly "emotional content, signaling both positive and negative appraisals." In terms of the benefit of such journal writing for teacher educators, Golombek and Doran (2014) noted that the dialogic interactions allowed the teacher educator to not only gain more insight into the reflections of the teachers but also become more self-reflective themselves. As Golombek and Doran (2014: 110) observed, "The iterative nature of writing and responding to reflection journals enables, even compels, teacher educators to engage in their own processes of self-reflection." However, they also suggest that other forms of mediation beyond written feedback may be necessary, such as face-to-face interactions and peer interactions to support the professional growth of novice teachers.

In a similar finding to the Golombek and Doran (2014) study above, Hernandez (2015) also reported on the benefits of reflective journal writing for both pre-service TESOL teachers and their teacher educators. Hernandez (2015) used regular reflection journals and a written report on an observed class to see how pre-service TESOL teachers could better understand SLA theory and observed that reflective writing provided valuable information about the impact of course materials and class activities to raise student teachers' awareness of their perceptions on SLA and on their philosophy of teaching. As Hernandez (2015: 147) remarked: "The use of reflective writings allowed documentation of participants' awareness of their role to bring about change in students' lives, thus confirming that personal practical knowledge has a moral and emotional dimension as well."

Golombek (2015) also reported on the use of reflection journals as a course requirement but this time the journals were not graded. The pre-service TESOL teachers were asked to write a journal each week and email it to the instructor who would respond to their individual journals via email. In this manner the instructor hoped to foster their reflections as well as learn about what they were thinking and experiencing as they wrote about their expectations of an internship they were about to take up and their strengths and concerns as they embarked on their learning-to-teach experience. Golombek (2015) reports specifically on the case of one pre-service TESOL teacher (Rose) and her initial hesitancy to openly express her opinion through writing, as she implied that her ideas would lose quality through her writing. According to Golombek (2015), this teacher considered such writing as "busy work" and even a "nuisance" and only wrote because she was asked to fulfill a course requirement as part of her internship. In fact, the teacher was more interested in face-to-face interactions, and she was, as Golombek (2015: 479) observed,

> Very much engaged in a dialogue of reflection in our face-to-face interactions, which she says she found most beneficial. Rose was exploiting our face-to-face interactions as a kind of spoken *narrative of externalization* in lieu of the journal.

Indeed, Golombek (2015) concluded that teacher educators must be aware of their own personal bias when promoting different instruments that they think may promote reflection because pre-service TESOL teachers may have different opinions, experiences and expectations; as Golombek (2015: 480) noted, "Rose as a learner needed to talk rather than write herself into thinking and reflecting." This is a similar finding to Farrell (2001) who suggested that the use of reflective practice instruments be tailored to individual TESOL teachers' needs, rather than those only promoted by teacher educators.

That said, most of the studies reviewed report that pre-service TESOL teachers are generally receptive to writing in journals to help foster reflective practice. According to Kömür and Çepik (2015), the pre-service TESOL teachers in their study liked writing because they said they could share their feelings and thoughts comfortably and freely in such a forum. Writing as reflection on their practice allowed them opportunities to apply their own experiences, values and beliefs in order to better evaluate what they had learned as well as obtain feedback from their teaching and learning processes. Tavil (2014) also used writing, but this time in electronic journals (or e-journals) to prompt pre-service TESOL teachers to reflect on their self-efficacy, and reported that such writing helped heighten their instructional efficacy. The pre-service TESOL teachers were very receptive to writing as reflection in this manner.

In an interesting study Kömür and Çepik (2015) asked their pre-service TESOL teachers to keep diaries outside of contact hours for the course on the subject of language learning and teaching so that they could reflect on their learning and teaching experiences. They noted that having pre-service TESOL teachers write outside the contact hours provided them with a summative document outlining the students' achievements and allowed them the freedom to discuss their views and ideas. In addition, the pre-service TESOL teachers were able to share their feelings and thoughts comfortably and more freely because it was outside regular contact hours.

Engin (2015) reported on the importance of written documents in post-observation discussions so as to maximize the learning and co-construction of meaning between facilitator and pre-service TESOL teachers. Engin (2015) suggests that written artifacts of a running commentary can play a crucial role in the dialogue between tutor and student teacher in a post-observation feedback session. As Engin (2015: 258) discovered, the written running commentary "can guide, constrain, and represent power and authority" in the post-observation conferences between student teacher and teacher educator. On the positive side, Engin (2015: 263) observed that running commentaries offer a written, tangible and permanent account of the lesson and can thus act as a "catalyst for discussion and reflection and provide a platform on which the pedagogic conversation can take place." In terms of constraints, Engin (2015) notes that the use of spatial deictic phrases can create a shared understanding of the context, but can also limit the discussion leading to limited critical reflection. In terms of power and authority, Engin (2015) points out too that reflection can be limited because the tutor is responsible for writing the artifact and thus controls the topics and order of questions.

For in-service TESOL teachers, journal writing was also a popular reflective instrument to aid their reflections. Chien (2013), for example, reported on a case study in detail of an elementary school EFL teacher's journal writing as reflective practice. Chien (2013) calculated that a total of 485 entries for 206 classes were written in one semester with the average of 2.35 entries per class and a maximum of five entries and a minimum of one entry per class. In addition, the most commonly reported issue in the journal entries was students' behavior (162 entries), followed by students' performance (155 entries), and teaching strategies (107 entries). The least reported issues were students with special needs (3 entries) and classroom management (8 entries). Such detail reported on the frequency and number of entries suggests, according to Chien (2013), that the journal itself became an excellent reflective practice instrument for the teacher to collect information about her teaching practice and examine her beliefs and assumptions in a more detailed manner. As Chien (2013: 139) observed: "The reflective practice through journal writing helped her examine her assumptions and beliefs as well as construct knowledge and improve her skills in terms of English teaching instructional strategies, classroom management issues, and students' English learning and performance." Writing regular journal entries according to Chien (2013), allowed the teacher to come up with her own solutions to problems that occurred and help her improve her practice.

Farrell (2013b) also reported on how regular journal writing facilitated one experienced ESL college teacher in Canada to reflect on her practice which resulted in a change of her perception of self as an ESL professional. Although the teacher was initially hesitant and apprehensive and even skeptical about writing as a process for reflection, Farrell (2013b) noted that the teacher reported that she came to enjoy it after her initial concern with having time to write. The writing process moved from an initial position of the teacher continually asking herself through her writing if her classes were effective, if her students enjoyed them and if they were successful or not, to a position where she noticed much more about her surroundings and became more confident about her practice. As Farrell (2013b: 470) remarked, writing helped the teacher to "first pause for a few moments to think about what she would actually write, and then reflect on that writing so she could understand and ultimately direct it to a place she wanted."

Genc (2010) noted the positive effect of regular journal writing for in-service TESOL teachers to become more aware of and understand their beliefs and knowledge about language learning and teaching. The teachers focused their reflections on problems related to lesson planning, the teaching/learning process, interaction, classroom management, and assessment. Genc (2010) maintained that writing regularly in journals helped the teachers become more aware and that this awareness was the first big step for them to think about possible solutions and to implement various teaching strategies they developed. As Genc (2010: 402) observed, writing as a process of reflection "was a kind of eye-opener because teachers felt empowered and autonomous in their classroom practices when they implemented self-initiated pedagogical options." The TESOL teachers were able to develop bottom-up teaching strategies based on the dynamics of their classrooms through critical reflection in journals because, according to Genc (2010), they were able to explore, analyze and observe their own beliefs and classroom practices, and experiment with alternative instructional behaviors. Genc (2010: 407) outlined the positive effects of journal writing for in-service TESOL teachers: The experience of keeping a reflective journal on their teaching helped the teachers in this study to:

- explore and analyze the factors affecting their instruction;
- become autonomous in restructuring teaching/learning processes in their contexts;
- gain the skills to go beyond language teaching methods and reflect on their practices in the classroom;
- be aware of and understand their own beliefs and knowledge about language learning/teaching;
- become more sensitive and respond effectively to their students' needs/ problems as language learners and develop appropriate teaching strategies;
- experience a bottom-up view of teaching.

However, not all in-service TESOL teachers were receptive to journal writing to help them reflect on their practice. Abednia, Hovassapian, Teimournezhad, and Ghanbari (2013) for example, encouraged in-service TESOL teachers to engage in journal writing to aid their reflections on practice. They were particularly interested in looking at the advantages and challenges of writing reflective journals. They incorporated reflective journal writing into the course and gave the TESOL teachers an opportunity to reflect on different aspects of their career and rethink their teaching beliefs and styles. The readings and class discussions acted as prompts for writing journals, since the readings would familiarize them with the professional literature of ELT and class discussions would provide them with an opportunity to share their understandings of the issues raised in the readings with each other and discuss them in light of their real-life language learning and teaching experiences. They discovered that the TESOL teachers considered such reflective journal writing as helpful for them to become more aware of their implicit beliefs about ELT and revisit them and improve their reasoning and self-expression skills. However, Abednia et al. (2013) also believed that writing put high demands on them in terms of preparatory readings prior to sessions and active involvement in class discussions. Also, they had to deal with the tension which arose between their schooling background and the reflective nature of journal writing. They suggested that they would need more guidance from course facilitators on the nature and process of reflective writing.

Reflective Questions

- How does writing help a teacher to reflect?
- What topics would you write about if asked to reflect on your practice? Do you think you would write about your feelings and emotions as one case study reported on or just your descriptions of your practice?
- Why do you think some pre-service TESOL teachers may view writing as "busy work" and even a "nuisance"?
- Several studies reported the benefits of having to provide written feedback for teacher educators because they must also engage in self-reflection. What is your understanding of this?
- One study noted that pre-service teachers were receptive to the idea of keeping diaries outside of contact hours. Why do you think this would be the case? Would you be receptive?
- A study reported that for one in-service teacher a journal itself became a way for the teacher to collect information about her teaching practice and examine her beliefs and assumptions in a more detailed manner. What is your understanding of this?
- Another study reported that journal writing allowed the teacher to first pause for a few moments to think about what she would actually write, and then reflect on that writing. What is your understanding of this?
- Comment on each of the following benefits for teachers of keeping a reflective journal on their teaching as reported in one study:

    a   explore and analyze the factors affecting their instruction;
    b   become autonomous in restructuring teaching/learning processes in their contexts;
    c   gain the skills to go beyond language teaching methods and reflect on their practices in the classroom;

d   be aware of and understand their own beliefs and knowledge about language learning/teaching;

e   become more sensitive and respond effectively to their students' needs/problems as language learners and develop appropriate teaching strategies;

f   experience a bottom-up view of teaching.

• Why do you think that not all pre-service or in-service TESOL teachers would like journal writing as a reflective instrument to help them reflect on their practice?

Classroom Observations

Classroom observations and follow-up video analysis were also used as reflective instruments to encourage TESOL teachers (both pre-service and in-service) to engage in reflective practice but not as frequently as the reflective practice instruments of discussion and writing. I present an analysis of classroom observations as they were used to foster reflection by pre-service TESOL teachers first and this is followed by in-service TESOL teachers.

Akcan (2010) for example, encouraged pre-service TESOL teachers to reflect on their teaching before, during and after classroom observations through the use of retrospective feedback sessions based on video-based reflections, in order to get candidates' opinions about how they felt while watching themselves during such observations. Akcan (2010) had 27 pre-service teachers view their video-recorded lessons with a university supervisor and they reflected together on the lesson in which feedback was also offered at the end of each viewing; in addition the teacher candidates reflected on the experience of observing their own teaching after the feedback sessions. Akcan (2010) reported that the pre-service TESOL teachers said that they had become more aware of their actual (rather than ideal) teaching practice and their use of English as well as gaining a better understanding of their students' behaviors. As Akcan (2010: 41) remarked, using such reflective tools as classroom observations and retrospective feedback helped the pre-service TESOL teachers "notice students' behaviors and responses (which may not have been noticed during the lesson because of the candidate's nervousness or anxiety), in analysing students' use of the target language, and in helping them to notice details of their own 'teacher talk.'" In such a manner, Akcan (2010) noted that these sources of reflective instruments allowed the pre-service TESOL teachers to step back and take a more critical stance about how they teach.

Eröz-Tuğa (2012) encouraged pre-service TESOL teachers to engage in self-reflection after classroom observations that were also video-taped. After classroom observations, Eröz-Tuğa (2012) encouraged the pre-service TESOL teachers to engage in self-evaluation through watching a video of their own teaching together with their university supervisor. Eröz-Tuğa (2012) observed that such a process helped the pre-service TESOL teachers become more insightful about their teaching practices. As Eröz-Tuğa (2012: 5) noted, the pre-service TESOL teachers "improved self-awareness and displayed a conscious effort in trying to fix the problems the [university supervisor] warned them about in the first feedback meeting, as well as the ones they noticed themselves. They were able to make comparisons between their first and second videos, pointing to improved aspects of their teaching performance as well as lingering weaknesses." In an insightful summary of this teacher growth, Eröz-Tuğa (2012: 7) observed:

In the first feedback session, almost all of the participants were somewhat reluctant about criticizing their own and their partners' performances; they mainly listened to the feedback of the university supervisor and took notes rigorously. Their comments predominantly focused on obvious classroom issues like tone of voice and body language, and they often overlooked critical issues, such as teaching inaccurate forms or time management. However, after the second video viewing, they were so expressive and accurate in their reflections and comments about the videos that the university supervisor did not need to go over all her notes; her points were all already covered by the students or their partner trainees.

Thus Eröz-Tuğa (2012) concluded that the classroom observations (and video of these classes) and feedback sessions had a positive impact on teachers' performance because they began to depend less on the feedback and more on their own interpretations of watching themselves on video teaching as they were able to take a more critical perspective.

Day (2013) also encouraged pre-service TESOL teachers to reflect on their practice, but rather than have supervisors provide feedback after the observation, he encouraged peers to observe each other and then give feedback to each other during their practicum. The peer observations consisted of four different stages: pre-observation conference, observation, post-observation conference, and peer observation report. Day (2013) reported positive findings to the use of such peer observations and observed that the teachers became more reflective and changed some of their teaching behaviors as a result of the peer feedback. Although Day (2013) noted that these changes cannot be directly linked to a new reflective stance on practice, the teachers themselves said that they would continue to use reflective teaching practices after the practicum. This shows, according to Day (2013), the importance of the impact of a reflective practicum on a future TESOL teacher's growth and development.

Regarding in-service TESOL teachers' use of classroom observations to promote reflection, Gun (2010) encouraged in-service teachers to video record their class and then to engage in post-lesson weekly discussions about their teaching. Gun (2010) reported that watching the video recording of the lessons and getting feedback on their teaching was very helpful for the teachers in nurturing critical reflection. However, Gun (2010: 7) noted that of all the different types of feedback, "watching videos of themselves teach was the most beneficial of all the feedback that came from different sources." Although the feedback obtained from colleagues, trainers and their students was very helpful for these experienced TESOL teachers, Gun (2010) observed that the video had the greatest impact because they knew what to watch out for in the videos and also identified other aspects of their practices that they needed to work on. Indeed, Gun (2010) pointed out the true value of the videos in nurturing reflective thinking because the teachers were able not only to identify potential areas of improvement as well as strengths, by watching videos of themselves, but also to transfer their critical reflection into "on the spot" strategies in their classroom and this appears to have greatly helped the teachers to become more autonomous, which is one of the tenets of engaging in reflective practice.

In an interesting and very comprehensive study of classroom observation, Lasagabaster and Sierra (2011) examined the perceptions of experienced TESOL teachers about classroom observation. I give this study a lot of detail in the review because it outlines how the researchers studied classroom observation in terms of three different components: a cognitive component, an affective component and a conative component, or the circumstances under which observation is to be implemented. This study has a lot to offer language teacher educators and developers when implementing classroom observations and in fact, outlines several important features necessary for the implementation of classroom observations that I detail later.

For the cognitive component, Lasagabaster and Sierra (2011) reported that the teachers said it was important in improving classroom teaching but they had differing preferences for different modes of observation (note taking, audio, video, etc.) and noted that this probably depends on the personality of the individual teacher being observed. Although most of the experienced TESOL teachers said observation could be beneficial because it can enhance awareness and allows for comparison of ideas, some also mentioned that it could be anxiety provoking and this leads to the introduction of the second component of analysis: the affective nature of classroom observations. Most of the 185 in-service TESOL teachers maintained that they felt uneasy about being watched while teaching and also worried about how the class would be affected and distracted. They noted that when choosing observers, they would prefer a colleague first and a trainer with linguistic expertise second, and this leads to the introduction of the final component of analysis: the conative component or the question of under what circumstances observation should be implemented. Over half of the teachers reported they would be willing to be observed because it would give them a chance to analyze their teaching, but nearly 40 percent still said they were reluctant to be observed. Thus Lasagabaster and Sierra (2011) maintain that for classroom observations to be implemented there is a need for a friendly, supportive environment, where there is empathy and trust between the observer and the observed, as well as mutual respect.

It should be noted that Lasagabaster and Sierra (2011: 454) cautioned that, although the majority of the in-service TESOL teachers agreed on the importance of observation, some teachers who had observed a fellow teacher assessed it positively because "it enhanced awareness" and allowed comparison of ideas. They noted that some other teachers were not always truthful in reporting because they did not want to be critical of the other teacher. The results of this study show that it is important to consider TESOL teachers' feelings about being observed and about giving and receiving feedback on teaching. Thus they maintain classroom observation should be voluntary. Lasagabaster and Sierra (2011) suggest the following features are necessary for successful classroom observations as gathered from the comments of the 187 in-service TESOL teachers in their study:

- Understand that observation takes up time.
- Observer should be inconspicuous and affect the class as little as possible.
- Establish clear objectives and procedures to follow from the beginning.
- Criticism should be constructive and the observer needs to remain objective about the work of the person being observed.
- The observer should be experienced and also familiar with the subject being taught.
- There needs to be co-ordination between the observer and the observed so that the findings can be talked about and assessed together.
- The observation process should not be an exercise detached from classroom reality.
- The observation has to be systematic, to avoid obtaining a distorted view of what happens in class and so that its benefits are tangible.
- Classroom observation must be voluntary.

In what could be seen as a follow-up to Lasagabaster and Sierra's (2011) study above, Ryder (2012) examined what type of in-service TESOL teachers welcome classroom observation and why, and if this leads to reflectivity. A total of 26 experienced TESOL teachers were invited to engage in classroom observations that would also include feedback sessions but only six teachers agreed to participate. Ryder (2012) discovered that remarks from those experienced TESOL teachers who declined to participate in any classroom observations cited a lack of time while others said that they felt no need for any help. The experienced TESOL teachers that participated in the classroom observations remarked that they thought it would be good for career advancement and professional status, and especially so because they were all contract teachers. In addition, these teachers reported that they were interested in knowing more about such classroom issues as meeting the needs of learners at different levels of proficiency and how to teach unmotivated students. Ryder (2012) reported that some teachers showed evidence of positive behavior changes as a result of the classroom observations but not all.

Reflective Questions

- How can classroom observation help TESOL teachers with self-reflection?
- How should classroom observation be carried out?
- Can and should TESOL teachers engage in classroom observation alone or with others? Explain your answer.
- What are the advantages and disadvantages of peer observations and peer feedback?
- One study reported that the pre-service TESOL teachers said that they had become more aware of their actual (rather than ideal) teaching. What is your understanding of this finding?
- One of the main issues reported with conducting successful classroom observations is the need for a friendly, supportive environment, where there is empathy and trust between the observer and the observed, as well as mutual respect. Why do you think this is the case?
- Comment on each of Lasagabaster and Sierra's (2011) main ingredients for successful classroom observations:

  a   Understand that observation takes up time.
  b   Observer should be inconspicuous and affect the class as little as possible.
  c   Establish clear objectives and procedures to follow from the beginning.
  d   Criticism should be constructive and the observer needs to remain objective about the work of the person being observed.
  e   The observer should be experienced and also familiar with the subject being taught.
  f   There needs to be co-ordination between the observer and the observed so that the findings can be talked about and assessed together.
  g   The observation process should not be an exercise detached from classroom reality.
  h   The observation has to be systematic, to avoid obtaining a distorted view of what happens in class and so that its benefits are tangible.
  i   Classroom observation must be voluntary.

- Why do you think one study discovered that for those teachers who declined to participate in any classroom observations, most cited a lack of time but some said that they felt no need for help (from observations) with their teaching?
- Why do you think becoming a more autonomous teacher (through engaging in classroom observations among other forms of reflection) is one of the tenets of engaging in reflective practice?

Action Research

Action research was also represented in the studies reviewed as a reflective practice instrument but much less frequently than discussion, writing and classroom observation. This is an interesting finding, given it is frequently being encouraged by teacher educators for both pre-service and in-service TESOL teachers. I present an analysis of action research as it was used to foster reflection by pre-service TESOL teachers first and this is followed by in-service TESOL teachers.

Cabaroglu (2014) was interested in finding out about pre-service TESOL teachers' teaching efficacy beliefs after their participation in action research and also sought to uncover what the teacher candidates thought about the action research process as related to their professional development. Cabaroglu (2014) looked at the results of 60 pre-service TESOL teachers' engagement in an action research project during a teacher education course which reported that such participation promoted reflective learning and deep thinking. Such positive effects reported by the pre-service TESOL teachers included increased sense of autonomy, creativity, reflectivity and confidence building. In addition, Cabaroglu (2014: 84) also noted that "a particular theme that echoed throughout the data was an improvement in teacher candidates' problem-solving skills, and as a result, in their teaching." The pre-service TESOL teachers also reported an increase in self-efficacy and that the action research project equipped them to face future teaching challenges.

Cutrim Schmid and Hegelheimer (2014) encouraged pre-service (and some in-service) TESOL teachers to engage in an action research project in conjunction with CALL course and technology-rich field experiences. In particular, according to Cutrim Schmid and Hegelheimer (2014), the pre-service TESOL teachers were required to carry out a small-scale research project, for which they needed to design, implement and evaluate at least four technology-enhanced lessons and write a research report on their findings. Each mini-research project followed the same structure and development. The first stage involved the investigation of the teachers' pedagogical practices. Data were collected through in-depth interviews (conducted mainly by the main researcher) and classroom observations (conducted by the students) for a period of one to three months. The students wrote down chronological descriptive field notes as the lessons unfolded. In the second stage, the students collaborated with the in-service teacher for the design, implementation and evaluation of at least four technology-enhanced lessons, which were video-recorded and later described in detail for further analysis. In order to better prepare the participating students for their research endeavors, a "young scientists research group" was set up by the main researcher. This group met once a month for a two-hour session. During these meetings the students received academic support on research methodology, exchanged ideas about their projects, and supported each other in research tasks such as narrowing down their research questions, designing questionnaires, coding research data, and so on. Cutrim Schmid and Hegelheimer (2014: 329) report positive effects of this use of action research, stating that "The results suggest that the field experiences, in conjunction with systematic guided reflection, have provided professional learning opportunities that supported the student teachers' development as CALL practitioners." In particular they noted that the pre-service TESOL teachers highlighted the benefit of engaging in action research that were implemented in the main framework of the program. As a result, they observed that incorporating a component of action research training into the program was a key element for its effective implementation and enabled the pre-service TESOL teachers to achieve a deeper understanding of CALL processes and outcomes.

Sowa (2009) was interested in encouraging pre-service TESOL teachers to reflect on their learners in order to get a better understanding of teaching linguistically diverse students. Sowa (2009) encouraged them to conduct action research projects together with course work in order to help these pre-service TESOL teachers learn more about their English language learners. Sowa (2009: 1029) reported that although most pre-service TESOL teachers reported that time was a challenge for them, and that most of them felt that there had not been enough time to see significant changes in their students, they still "felt conducting action research projects in this class had given them the tools to conduct small research projects in their classrooms and to share their ideas with colleagues." The pre-service teachers said that their action research projects had helped them gain an understanding of their students, make them become more aware of how and what they were teaching and, as a result, their teaching had changed somewhat. Sowa (2009: 1030) observed that the pre-service TESOL teachers had all become more reflective:

> The data showed that reflection was a crucial factor contributing to the changes in their teaching. All the teachers noted that their experiences had made them more reflective and critical about their teaching. This in turn had led to a change in their teaching, as well as their ideas about teaching ELLs in particular and all students in general.

Because they had become more reflective from conducting the action research projects, the pre-service TESOL teachers said they felt they had grown as teachers, and were more confident about teaching ELLs. In particular, Sowa (2009: 1031) remarked that for these pre-service TESOL teachers, "conducting action research projects helped [them] to start reflecting more critically about their practice particularly with respect to strategies they teach in the classroom to help all students learn." In the future, the teachers also noted that conducting the projects helped them develop skills needed to investigate and analyze challenges they may face in their classrooms.

With regard to in-service TESOL teachers being encouraged to engage in action research, many studies (too many to cover them all here) reported on the positive effects of conducting action research. For example, Banegas et al. (2013) is perhaps most representative of the positive effects of encouraging in-service TESOL teachers to conduct action research projects as part of their reflecting on practice. They noted that in-service TESOL teachers benefit enormously from involvement in action research and especially for their focus on the integration of content and language. Not only that, they also reported that such an approach to the in-service TESOL teachers' professional development through action research impacted their students' motivation to learn English more positively, which is the real benefit of engaging in such projects. As Banegas et al. (2013: 193) remark, engaging in action research "stimulated deeper reflection and awareness of teaching practices" and initiated some changes in teaching styles and practices. As a result of such an approach to their professional development through reflective practice via conducting action research, the teachers became more aware of their practices and the impact of their teaching on their students' motivation to learn. As Banegas et al. (2013: 191) observed, there was a "dynamic relationship between student motivation and teacher motivation and autonomy."

It is interesting to note that for many of the studies related to in-service TESOL teachers engaging in action research, many of the projects were large in nature and attempted to connect this action research with overall teacher research and also university researchers in some manner. It is also interesting to note that many of these large-scale projects reported some tensions and complexities (more than with pre-service TESOL teachers) associated with their construction and development, especially in the eyes of the in-service teachers who felt they are disenfranchised in some manner.

Chan (2015), for example, in a large-scale school-university action research project, examined a research project that was designed to help English language teachers develop the skills needed to deal with the reforms to assessment practices in Hong Kong's school curriculum. In this project, the in-service TESOL teachers chose their own research focus, interventions and data collection methods. The teacher educators provided regular online support to help the teachers implement two cycles of action research over a six-month period. There were also three face-to-face meetings. Email was the preferred mode of communication, as the teachers were busy. The support provided by the teacher educators included helping the teachers to identify their research focus, co-planning the action research and assisting in the data collection process. Chan (2015) reported that this was a complex research project and tensions arose between university facilitators and the in-service teachers because of perceived power differentials. As Chan (2015: 121) noted, "shared power and equity were not achieved in this project" because social relationships were "hierarchical in the sense that the teachers expected the facilitators to 'author-rise' their ideas for the action research project." It seems then that in this study the in-service TESOL teachers considered that the university researchers had in some manner co-opted their research rather than negotiating with the teachers about their interests. Thus, Chan (2015) concluded that collaboration must be an ongoing process of negotiation and that collaboration between schools and university cannot be constructed outside and beyond relations of power.

Connected to the findings that some in-service TESOL teacher research may be co-opted by university researchers is the pressure put on some teachers to publish the results of their research by these supervisors and/or facilitators. Gao, Barkhuizen, and Chow (2011) for example, examined in-service TESOL teachers' perceptions of conducting action research projects and how they considered such research should be focused. Gao, Barkhuizen, and Chow (2011) noted that the teachers said they were more concerned about improving their practice with such research rather than with any publication of that research. In fact, they noted that publication is not always necessary for the research to be successful. Gao, Barkhuizen, and Chow (2011) remarked that the teachers pointed out that they knew there would be a lack of financial support for their efforts and some cited their low motivation connected to their uncertainties with their writing skills when trying to publish in a highly selective environment.

Thus in order to make such teacher research more appealing and successful, Yuan and Lee (2015) suggest that teacher research can be facilitated and enhanced by scaffolding provided by the university researchers. The teachers' research in this case as Yuan and Lee (2015: 3) point out, was aimed at solving "practical problems and improve the effectiveness of their teaching." Yuan and Lee (2015) explained that the teachers and researchers, each with clearly defined responsibilities (as outlined below), set out to learn from (rather than co-opt or compete with) each other and reflect on and enhance their professional practice through reflection and research. Here the university researchers served as facilitators who not only organized various professional activities (for example seminars and project meetings) to enhance the teachers' knowledge of research, but also offered scaffolding for teachers to help them deal with the obstacles in their research. More importantly, according to Yuan and Lee (2015), the researchers served as collaborators by sharing their research expertise and perspectives, and encouraging teachers to take on the role of reflective practitioners. Yuan and Lee (2015) reported that the scaffolding provided by the university team helped the teachers cope with many noted obstacles when teachers are asked to conduct action research such as time constraints, a lack of collegial support, and a rigid curriculum. In addition, the scaffolding process changed the teachers' understanding of research; as Yuan and Lee (2015: 5) observed: "The scaffolding provided by the university researchers played a crucial role in challenging the teachers' original beliefs about research. At the beginning of the project, the teachers lacked knowledge of (action) research and how it could be integrated into teaching, thinking that research was very remote from their classroom practice." Yuan and Lee (2015) concluded that such guidance and support from researchers may be necessary to help teachers how to successfully integrate action research into their practice, especially when faced with such contextual obstacles as time constraints, a lack of collegial support, and a rigid curriculum.

Kayaoglu (2015) also examined if action research may be a viable option for in-service TESOL teacher development while in their schools, and reported that they changed their initial negative views of action research to a more positive view after they were instructed as to how they could conduct such research. As

Kayaoglu (2015: 156) remarked, "Once encouraged to look at classroom happenings or practice critically, the teachers in this research were found to bring about change in the practice." Because they were instructed in how to conduct action research, the teachers reported that they found action research a valuable tool for reflection on different aspects of their practice so that they could develop professionally. In addition, and similar to what Yuan and Lee (2015) report above about change agents, the teachers in this study also perceived themselves as agents of change. As Kayaoglu (2015: 157) observed, the "teachers came to view themselves as agents of change in improving practice because it is the teacher who, of his/her own will, gets involved in critical reflection, evaluation, and action based on the evidence collected."

Reflective Questions

- How can conducting action research projects help pre-service TESOL teachers to face future teaching challenges?
- One study reported on different stages an action research project for pre-service TESOL teachers followed such as: 1) investigation of the teachers' pedagogical practices, data collection (interviews and classroom observations and field notes; 2) design, implementation and evaluation of lessons (video-recorded and later described in detail for further analysis); 3) monthly group meetings (on research methodology, exchange ideas about their projects, and support – designing questionnaires, coding research data). Comment on this approach to conducting action research for pre-service TESOL teachers.
- How can pre-service TESOL teachers conduct action research on their learners in order to get a better understanding of teaching linguistically diverse students? What can they learn from engaging in such research?
- Some studies of in-service TESOL teachers conducting action research projects in their school report some tensions, especially between university-based researchers and the teachers. Why would this be the case?
- How can action research be best facilitated and enhanced with school-university partnerships?
- How can university researchers support in-service TESOL teachers in their action research engagement?
- How would you instruct in-service TESOL teachers to conduct action research in their schools?

Narrative Study

The final reflective instrument discussed in this chapter is narrative study, which was used to enable TESOL teachers to reflect on their practice, but not as much as the other instruments outlined above. Therefore, it will be outlined and discussed in brief compared to those other reflective instruments. Narrative as a reflective tool for encouraging pre-service TESOL teachers to reflect on their practice was used powerfully by Barkhuizen (2010) to facilitate the identity development of a pre-service TESOL teacher. More specifically, Barkhuizen (2010) encouraged the pre-service TESOL teacher to make use of what he called "small stories-in-interaction" to help her answer the question "Who am I?" As a result, he noted that the teacher could use the story to dissect her forming identity as a teacher. As Barkhuizen (2010: 296) noted: "through making sense of her own claims about identity in the small story, as articulated in my analysis, she is now able to re-story her experiences of becoming a language teacher; and with each re-storying continue repositioning and reimagining her own teacher identity."

For in-service TESOL teachers, most studies reported positive effects of using narrative study to help facilitate reflection. Shelley, Murphy, and White (2013) for example, used a narrative framework successfully to enable distance language teachers to outline and reflect on their experience. A narrative frame consists of a set of incomplete sentences that teachers must complete, and as Barkhuizen and Wette (2008: 376) note, "provide guidance and support in terms of both the structure and content" of what is to be filled in in a type of story template.

Shelley, Murphy, and White (2013: 572) reported that the participants said that they found the "open structure of the narrative frame questionnaire accessible, thought-provoking and professionally rewarding."

Although not as frequently used as a reflective practice instrument to facilitate reflections, I included narrative study because a further analysis of the studies on the practices that encourage TESOL teachers, both pre-service and in-service, to reflect on their work show an increasing use of this tool to help prompt reflections. Perhaps future researchers can monitor the growing popularity with this excellent reflective instrument in the coming years.

Reflective Questions

- How would telling your story be a powerful way of reflecting on the professional identity of a pre-service teacher?
- What is your understanding of "re-storying" as a means of engaging in narrative study of a teacher's reflections?
- Why would narrative frames that consist of a set of incomplete sentences that teachers must complete help in-service TESOL teachers to reflect on their professional identity and their overall development as a TESOL teacher?
- Why do you think narrative study as a reflective tool to help facilitate TESOL teachers' reflections is growing in popularity?

Conclusion

This chapter outlined and discussed the main reflective practice instruments or tools used to encourage and facilitate reflection in the studies that were reviewed.

In order of the most frequently used, discussion (including teacher discussion groups and post-observation conferences) was the most frequently used in this body of research, followed by writing, closely followed by classroom observations (self, peer, etc., with or without video/audio), and then by lesser frequency action research. Less frequently used were narrative and lesson study. Reflective instruments such as cases, portfolio, team teaching, peer coaching, and critical friend/incident transcript reflections were used three or fewer times in the review studies. It should also be noted that there was some overlap between the use of many of the reflective instruments in some of the studies but for the most part, the results stand as outlined above. That said, the studies do not really make any particular case as to why one instrument would be preferred to another and just reported their usage of a particular reflective instrument to enable both pre-service and in-service TESOL teachers to reflect. In fact, one of the shortcomings that I have noted in this presentation of the reflective instruments used in many of the reviewed studies is that on closer inspection the accounts of the use of these instruments do not provide precise descriptions of practices in terms of the procedures or approaches to guide implementation of such instruments. So with that in mind, I attempted to provide examples of studies above that provided as much detail as possible when using such reflective instruments. The chapter that follows provides an overall appraisal of the reviewed studies on the practices that encourage TESOL teachers to reflect.

9

APPRAISAL

Introduction

In the previous chapters I presented a review of research on reflective practice from 138 research studies on the practices that encourage TESOL teachers to engage in reflect practice. The results of this review are overwhelmingly positive regarding the transformative potential and developmental benefits of encouraging TESOL teachers to engage in reflective practice. Such reflections can lead to enhanced awareness of important issues for both pre-service and in-service TESOL teachers such as reflection on their philosophy, principles, theory, and practice and beyond practice. Because of this enhanced awareness, both pre-service and in-service TESOL teachers can become more empowered to not only reflect on their practice but also be transformed so that they can provide optimum learning opportunities for their students, which after all is one of the main purposes for teachers engaging in reflective practice. This chapter thus provides a general appraisal (in addition to evaluations within each of the chapters so far) of the research results that were presented in the previous chapters through the lens of the framework for reflecting on practice. The chapter first outlines and discusses the participants, context and setting and this is followed by definitions, then methodology and instruments, with final reflections on the appraisal.

Participants, Context, Setting

The 138 studies reviewed seemed to be evenly divided between pre-service and in-service TESOL teachers with only a few studies having both pre-service and in-service teachers as participants. In particular, 65 studies were of pre-service TESOL teachers' reflections, 64 studies were of in-service TESOL teachers' reflections, while nine studies could be classified as both pre-service and in-service. That nearly 50 percent of all the studies reviewed in the preceding chapters focused on the practices that encouraged in-service/experienced TESOL teachers to reflect contradicts what some scholars have recently suggested about the paucity of reflective practice research related to in-service/experienced teachers' reflections on their work (e.g., Borg, 2011b; Mann & Walsh, 2013). Borg (2011b) for example, although not actually criticizing reflective practice research outright, nevertheless remarked that the reflections of in-service, experienced TESOL teachers does not reflect their actual circumstances or their realities of practice. As Borg (2011b: 220) maintained, "the literature [on reflective practice in TESOL] is insufficiently grounded in the realities that language teachers work in, and a closer empirical analysis of these realities is required before reflective practice can become a viable global strategy for LTE [language teacher education] (especially in in-service contexts)." This point can now be disputed as it is clear from the studies reviewed in this book that the practices that encourage in-service, experienced TESOL teachers to reflect are highly context related and contain the teachers' realities of practice both inside and outside their classrooms and in most global settings. I would suggest then that reflective practice research related to both pre-service and in-service TESOL teachers has already become a global strategy of practice (see also section below on settings of studies reviewed) and as such, language teacher educators must consider making it a specific strategy of practice rather than a referral, i.e., asking teachers to just "reflect on this or that" without any adherence to any underpinning theory of what defines "reflect," which is to me the most important issue related to the use of reflection in language teacher education programs today (see Chapter 2 on definitions).

In terms of the context of where the studies took place, globally Asia was the most represented with 52 studies or 37 percent, followed by Europe with 27 studies, then North America with 25 studies, Middle East 15 studies, Australia/New Zealand ten studies, South America six studies, and Africa three studies. In addition, most of the studies were located in tertiary level institutions at the graduate level followed closely by undergraduate programs and a few certificate programs. Regarding studies related to in-service TESOL teachers' engagement in reflective practice, Asia again leads the way with 28 studies represented in the review, or 43 percent, followed by Europe with 13 studies, the Middle East with 11 studies, North America with ten studies, South America with two studies, and New Zealand with one study. In addition, similar to the studies related to the setting of pre-service TESOL teachers, most were located in tertiary level institutions but unlike pre-service teachers, there were more studies located in certificate-type courses in public and private institutions. Given the wide geographical scope covered by the studies reviewed in this book, it seems that reflective practice has become a viable global strategy for LTE (language teacher education) for both pre-service and in-service TESOL teachers as part of their overall professional development.

In terms of the setting of the studies reviewed, the results suggest that not many studies are conducted outside various university programs and one may wonder what impact this has on the reflection processes in terms of the reflective objectives teachers are encouraged to reflect on as well as the reflective tools they are exposed to (this is addressed in more detail below under Objectives).

The results from an analysis of participants, context and setting indicate that there is an even distribution of the studies between pre-service and in-service TESOL teachers' engagement in reflective practice which counteracts claims made by some TESOL scholars that reflective practice is only prevalent in pre-service teacher education courses and that the experiences of the reflections of in-service TESOL teachers are not well represented. In addition, in terms of the setting of these studies, the results indicate that nearly half of all the studies reviewed were from Asian contexts, followed by less than a quarter conducted in Europe and North America and then far fewer in the Middle East, Australia and New Zealand, and very few conducted in South America and Africa. Furthermore, most studies reviewed were in some manner connected to university or college programs, such as under-graduate, graduate or language school programs, with only a few studies located within language schools, or primary, elementary or secondary school settings.

However, with the results of the analysis of the site of the studies that clearly favor university type sites/programs, we must ask the question of how this type of site frames the reflective practice process and if this provides opportunities for both pre-service TESOL teachers and in-service teachers to reflect or impedes their ability to reflect. For example, because most studies covered in this review were conducted in some kind of university context, we can wonder what reflective practices have been encouraged or adapted within these contexts where teacher educators pursue an intellectual approach to reflective practice in a "one size fits all" approach, while ignoring the inner life of teachers (I will return to this issue under objectives below).

Reflective Questions

- Why do you think some TESOL scholars would suggest that in-service TESOL teachers' realities have not been studied or scrutinized within the umbrella of reflective practice?
- Following your reading of the contents of the previous chapters, would you say that this is still the case?
- Do you think that reflective practice research has now become a viable global strategy for LTE (language teacher education) for both pre-service and in-service TESOL teachers as part of their overall professional development? Why or why not?
- In terms of engagement in the practices that encourage TESOL teachers to reflect, why do you think that Asia was most represented in this review?
- Why do you think there is less interest in reflective practice research in North America and Europe?

- Why do you think that a university setting was most prevalent in terms of location of most of the reviewed studies?
- How do you think that TESOL teachers can be encouraged to engage in more reflective practice research in their own schools?

Definitions

In terms of definitions of reflection and reflective practice as indicated in Chapter 2, only 52 of the 138 studies attempted to define the terms they had mentioned, such as reflection and reflective practice, which means we do not know how to classify the remaining 75 who did not define their terms or the 11 who vaguely defined their terms. This results in our lack of clarity in understanding the studies' underpinning theoretical positions. Thus I had to find a different manner of "understanding" what the articles referred to when they used all the different terms and the meanings they implied as there was no correspondence I could see between the usage and the research that was conducted that encouraged the teachers to engage in reflective practice. Consequently, I attempted to examine the different philosophical underpinnings and motivations behind the concepts used. As Akbari, Behzadpoor, and Dadvand (2010) have noted, because reflection as a concept has been influenced by different philosophies and motivations in its genesis, it makes an exact definition of the term problematic. The most popular components of reflective practice were cognitive followed by metacognitive and practical, then a long way back, critical, learner and moral. I mentioned in Chapter 1 that ultimately it is up to each teacher and teacher educator to define what reflection and reflective practice means to them and that we must be cautious about hasty referencing of a particular scholar's work on reflective practice without a full understanding or critical examination of its meaning.

For example, I outlined what and who has shaped my definitions of reflective practice: one reason why I think Dewey and Schön have influenced my own thoughts on this complex concept is that they are both pragmatic because they view reflection as grounded in practice (although Dewey worked mostly with teachers, while Schön did not). For Dewey, when the reflective practitioner encounters some problem while teaching, he or she must interrupt that teaching in order to solve the problem (through engaging in five steps of reflective inquiry). When he or she has solved that problem, the teacher can then resume action. However, Schön sees no need to suspend the action; rather the reflective practitioner can reflect during that action when confronted with anything that seems to be different from usual within the action. This sets off a causal reflective chain that ends similar to Dewey with teachers stepping back to reflect on the action. I agree with both approaches but have moved towards a more holistic view of reflection where the person as teacher is included (emotions, morals, ethics etc.) in the reflective process (*In* and *On* Action) and where the context can also shape the reflective process.

Therefore, when TESOL teachers are encouraged to reflect, either generally in a language teacher education program or in in-service courses, they should know in whose tradition this reflection is mirrored (i.e., is it Deweyan, Schönian, or a TESOL scholar – as the 138 studies show, we now have enough studies within TESOL to cite) because they must have a full understanding of that approach and its theoretical underpinning to make sure it aligns with what *they* think reflection and reflective practice is. It is important then for language teacher educators to allow time for teachers in training and in-service to define and discuss their understanding of reflection rather than being just told to "reflect." Of course this also means that language teacher educators must themselves take time to consider their own understanding of reflection. My hope is that as a profession we avoid reducing reflection and reflective practice to narrow focused recipe-following checklists that teachers fill in to satisfy the needs of teacher educators. We must consider TESOL teachers' personal histories, beliefs, theories and expectations for practice and beyond practice which may differ from those of language teacher educators, otherwise reflection and reflective practice will become a mechanical and ritualistic tool to fulfill the needs of administrators and teacher educators rather than the needs of TESOL teachers. I return to this issue at the end of this chapter.

Reflective Questions

Carl Rodgers (2002: 843) has observed some important issues associated with a lack of a clear definition of reflection that is pertinent to this discussion and thus I end this section by encouraging TESOL teachers and teacher educators to reflect on these important questions:

- It is unclear how systematic reflection is different from other types of thought. Does mere participation in a study group, or keeping a journal, for example, qualify as reflection?
- If a teacher wants to think reflectively about or inquire into her practice, what does she do first? How does she know if she is getting better at it? To what should she aspire?
- How do we assess this skill of reflection, as it is vaguely defined?
- Are personal ruminations enough or are there specific criteria for reflection?
- How does the lack of a common language mean that talking about it is either impossible, or practitioners find themselves using terms that are common but hold different meanings or are different but have overlapping meanings (e.g. reflection, inquiry, critical thinking, metacognition)?
- Without a clear sense of what we mean by reflection, do you think it is difficult to research the effects of reflective teacher education and professional development (e.g., inquiry groups, reflective journals, or book clubs) on teachers' practice and students' learning?

Methodology

Mann and Walsh (2013) have maintained that there is a scarcity of what they call "data-led" research on reflective practice. Mann and Walsh (2013: 292) continue, "There is a lack of data-led research on RP and a need for data-led practice in RP [reflective practice]. Put simply, we need more evidence from the perspectives of both research and professional development." When examining all 138 journal articles for methodological approaches, we can see that 70% of all studies, or 97 studies, took an overall qualitative approach, and only four studies were quantitative in nature with 37 studies using both for a mixed-method approach. In fact, when examined through a focus on pre-service and in-service TESOL teachers exclusively, 44 studies took a qualitative approach, and only four studies were quantitative in nature with 17 studies using both for a mixed-method approach but for in-service, 48 studies took a qualitative approach, 16 a mixed-method approach but no studies took a quantitative approach.

Perhaps the results above indicate an over-reliance on case studies and non-qualitative methods and this can be viewed as a shortcoming; however, as van Lier (2005: 195) has noted, case studies are better able to track changes in human behavior in a way that "cannot be adequately researched in any of the other common research methods." That said, for the mixed-method approach where both quantitative and qualitative methods were used, many studies proceeded in a common pattern of two different phases where the first phase consisted of quantitative analysis that included descriptive statistics (frequency distribution, means and standard deviations) calculated in order to prepare in some manner for the second more qualitative phase that may have included questionnaires/surveys, interviews, observations and their analysis/interpretation and other such probes that numbers may not be able to reveal.

Both approaches have strengths and weaknesses, but rather than giving any opinion about which approach is better, I would suggest that perhaps many of the types of studies conducted in this review of the practices that encourage TESOL teachers to reflect would lend themselves to qualitative approaches, where qualities or characteristics of issues (e.g., human behavior such as emotions, personality and the like) would not be presented better in numerical form that the more quantitative approaches prefer and where size of samples is more important. It will be interesting to see what approaches are most commonly used in future research on the practices that encourage TESOL teachers to reflect.

Reflective Questions

- How would you define data-led research on reflective practice?
- Do you think that the studies reviewed in this book can be considered data-led research on reflective practice? Explain your answer.

- Why do you think some TESOL scholars would suggest there were not enough data-led research studies related to reflective practice in TESOL?
- Following your reading of the contents of the previous chapters, would you say that this is still the case?
- Why do you think most of the research methodology centered on qualitative approaches?
- What is your understanding of a mixed-method approach to research in reflective practice?
- Why do you think there were no quantitative approaches to research at the in-service or more experienced TESOL teacher level?
- What are the strengths and weaknesses of quantitative, qualitative, and mixed-methods when it comes to designing research on the practices that encourage TESOL teachers to reflect on their practice?

Objectives

In terms of reflection objectives, overall results suggest a positive impact of encouraging pre-service and in-service TESOL teachers to reflect on their work, be it solely on their *philosophy, principles, theory, practice* and *beyond practice*, and/or their various combinations, all of which were covered in this review.

For example, when TESOL teachers were encouraged to reflect on their *philosophy* (mostly through accessing their personal histories) most studies reported that teachers can better understand their teacher identity origins, formation and development. The results of reflection on philosophy indicated that for pre-service TESOL teachers identity construction was very important and that different types of discourse and reflection can help pre-service teachers to shape, reshape and make sense of their teaching identities. With such discussions and reflection in the form of imagined identities, pre-service TESOL teachers can prepare more realistically for their future careers as they can be encouraged to reflect on their imagined future working life within an imagined community of teachers and English language learners. One case study for example (Barkhuizen, 2010) outlined such a situation in detail and reported on the reflections of a teacher on her identity where she was then able to (re)evaluate and rethink ideas about teaching and her imagined roles within teaching and learning communities as she began her transformation from a peripheral member of the community of teachers (and learners) of English into a more legitimate future participant of that community.

For those pre-service TESOL teachers who move contexts, usually to a country different from their place of origin to study and/or work as a TESOL teacher, the idea of shifting identities was highlighted and, as a result, such knowledge of the idea of shifting identities for pre-service TESOL teachers who move back and forth between countries will be important for language teacher education programs to consider. As Kong (2014: 91) points out, teacher education programs should "provide reflective activities to help pre-service

TESOL teachers understand and cope with the shifting of identity that will inevitable occur."

Indeed, one particular study (Kanno & Stuart, 2011) suggested that TESOL teacher learning is not so much the acquisition of the knowledge of language teaching methodology and skills as it is the development of a teacher identity. This study also argues that the acquisition of knowledge (perhaps content knowledge and pedagogical knowledge) is part of this identity development, but not the other way around.

Studies related to in-service TESOL teacher reflections on philosophy and its various combinations revealed the idea of an identity gap that can exist between what teachers felt they were expected to become (i.e., "designated teacher identity") and how they realistically identified themselves (i.e., "actual teacher identity"). Thus by being encouraged to engage in reflective practice, the in-service TESOL teachers began to notice the gap and as a result shifted their identity (especially where there were competing identities at play) to adapt to different situations, based on many rounds of reinterpretation of the self and the situation. Studies revealed that in-service TESOL teachers noted that in this relational process, a gap was always present between the teacher's designed identity (identity that is dictated by the dominant discourse of the community and a novice teacher feels "bound" to follow) and actual identity (identity that is not bound and a novice teacher is free to develop her or his own persona). To close this gap, as Liu and Xu (2011: 594) noted, teachers engage in a process of making and remaking identity by using different "positioning strategies based on the situational meanings that she derived from the context."

Most of the studies on this objective of philosophy were in the form of story sharing and re-storying and by sharing their stories, TESOL teachers can come to understand the importance of thinking critically regarding their identity (origin, formation and development) and so they can move forward from these reflections to seek out what Morgan (2009: 89) has suggested are the "possibilities for transformative work at the micro level of the classroom."

When teachers were encouraged to reflect on *principles* (mostly through metaphor analysis and reflective writing), most (but not all) studies reviewed reported that teachers became more aware of their previously tacitly held assumptions, values and beliefs about teaching and learning, and as a result, they were better able to re-evaluate them in light of their new knowledge.

An important issue that arose in the studies related to both pre-service and in-service TESOL teachers' reflecting on their beliefs, is that many struggle to articulate and externalize these tacitly held assumptions and beliefs, a common issue in the literature on teacher beliefs (see Senior, 2006 for more on this). Not only are they difficult to articulate, but once articulated some TESOL teachers also discover that they are very complex and difficult to understand (Farrell & Bennis, 2013; Farrell & Ives, 2015). That said, many, pre-service and in-service TESOL teachers using reflective tools such as metaphor analysis, action research projects, post-observation conferences and video prompts reported that the teachers felt liberated when they articulated their beliefs and were then able to make specific modifications or even completely change their beliefs.

When teachers were encouraged to reflect on *theory* (mostly through lesson planning) the studies reported that pre-service TESOL teachers were able to build repertoires and knowledge of instruction while in-service TESOL teachers benefited most from accessing their theory though collective and collaborative lesson-planning conferences.

Many of the reviewed studies revealed that the main result of these reflections was the pre-service TESOL teachers' growing awareness of the needs of their students rather than their own need to survive when they took different approaches to planning for teaching. In addition, many of these studies highlighted the use of collaborative lesson planning as a means of encouraging the TESOL pre-service TESOL teachers to engage in such reflections and as a result of such reflections they were able to identify important issues related to planning, propose specific actions that would enable successful lessons, and evaluate these in light of imagined classroom events. In this manner many studies revealed that the teachers (pre-service and in-service) were able to better understand and see other perspectives rather than their own.

As mentioned in Chapter 5, there were no clear instances where the teachers just focused their reflections on their practice exclusively without combining these reflections with other aspects of the framework, such as theory, but in a subordinate role. It is interesting to note that such a combination of practice and theory accounted for nearly 40 percent of all studies reviewed (as such I give it more coverage in this section of the appraisal).

When pre-service TESOL teachers were encouraged to reflect on this combination, the results indicated that some kind of feedback during pre-and post-observation conferences in groups of some form (e.g., with or without video recordings of the lessons) can facilitate such reflections. One reason for the necessity of some guidance and feedback for these pre-service TESOL teachers on reflections of theory and practice is that they are full of self-blame initially; however, whenever guidance and feedback is provided, even of a general nature, studies show that the pre-service TESOL teachers seemed to make clearer connections between theory and practice. Thus it seems that some form of intervention may be necessary to help pre-service TESOL teachers reflect at this level. Such guidance, however, should prioritize the pre-service TESOL teachers' perspectives so as to invite reflection and thus take a "solution-attentive approach" rather than a "cause-attentive approach," as the latter can put the pre-service teacher on the defensive rather than fostering a real understanding of the issue.

Another important issue that arose for pre-service TESOL teachers reflecting with a supervisor on their theory and practice was that of power relations and the fact that many such reflections involve the use of written artifacts (such as a teaching evaluation form or a teaching write up) as a platform for pedagogic conversations about practice. The issue here is that the teacher educator/supervisor usually has sole authority when filling it in. Thus some studies suggest that a video-recording component be added as a way around the issue of power relations because such video-recording feedback sessions are less dependent on peers and supervisor for feedback and reflection (see Eröz-Tuğa, 2012 for more on this).

Yet another important issue that arose when pre-service TESOL teachers reflect on their theory and practice in teacher education programs was the issue of grading. Results indicated that when pre-service teachers gained a high academic grade within their teacher education courses, this high grade was not translated into high teaching performance when the pre-service TESOL teachers were encouraged to reflect on the impact of their planning on their teaching and vice versa; as Yesilbursa (2011b: 179) pointed out, "high academic performance may not always entail practical expertise or the potential for creative reflection with an open mind." This conclusion, although acknowledged by many teacher educators and teachers alike has not been given enough attention in the language teacher education literature.

A related problem connected to language teacher education programs and courses was that as a result of their reflections on their teaching practice, the pre-service TESOL teachers expressed a concern about the inconsistency between theory provided in teacher education programs and actual experiences of practice. So they highlighted a need for more practice in the methodology courses in their teacher education program. Such reflections have implications for TESOL teacher education courses and I have already written about this in a different collection (see Farrell (2015c) for more on this topic).

When in-service TESOL teachers are encouraged to reflect on this combination, results indicate that although most teachers report an overall positive impact of classroom observations because they lead to enhanced awareness of theory and practice connections, they also noted the potential adverse reactions to being observed by others, so the affective side of classroom observations should be considered. Thus the results also reveal that other forms of post-observation feedback such as the use of teacher groups, teacher study groups or critical friends, may not only stimulate reflection on theory/practice connections but also alleviate some of the affective issues and misgivings about being observed.

Other combinations of reflection included explorations of *principles, theory and practice*, which added more detail on connections between assumptions, beliefs, and lesson planning and their relation to classroom practices. Similar to the previous combination of reflections on theory and practice was the importance of post-observation conferences, but with a majority of these conducted through some kind of online mode of reflection such as forums, chats and blogs. Indeed, when in-service TESOL teachers were encouraged to reflect specifically on the connection between beliefs, theory and practice, the teachers reported not only an increased awareness of the complex connection within this combination but also the possibility of discrepancy between all three.

Although few studies resulted in reflection beyond practice as in the combination of *principles, theory, practice and beyond practice*, of those that did, most noted that both pre-service and in-service TESOL teachers were not only able to reflect on their own assumptions, beliefs, and theories and how they could use this information to improve their practice, but also beyond practice and how these are all connected to wider school and social issues. Indeed, as one study noted, such critical reflection allowed the TESOL teachers to go beyond language instruction and fulfill educationally oriented promises such as helping people become critical thinkers and active citizens.

When in-service TESOL teachers were encouraged to reflect beyond practice in combination with philosophy, principles, theory and practice, most of the studies reported that the teachers reflected well beyond their classroom teaching practices on such issues as the textbooks they are given to teach, the syllabus and curriculum they are given and their working conditions, especially what they are expected to do by the administration rather than what they think their professional roles are.

These results of the analysis of the overall reflections of TESOL teachers throughout the framework suggest then that the main focus of their reflections tends to be on more practical and immediate issues related to their classroom practices, but not much on themselves (philosophy) or beyond their classroom (critical reflection). Thus it may be an idea for teacher educators and TESOL teachers to be encouraged to expand their reflections on their philosophy so that they know who they are as a teacher-as-person. They can also be encouraged to reflect beyond the classroom to encourage the greater socio-cultural context in which they find themselves teaching. Perhaps the best way is to encourage teachers (and teacher educators) to reflect on all aspects of the framework for reflecting on practice and see how all stages interact and impact each other so that these reflections show a complete person-as-reflective practitioner.

One way teacher educators and teacher education programs can expand their TESOL teachers' reflections to include philosophy and beyond practice as some studies suggest, is to incorporate some kind of community-based service learning project (that integrates classroom instruction with community service activities) into TESOL teacher preparation courses. Such a course can have TESOL teachers reflect on who they are as practitioners as well as what they stand for outside their classrooms. Indeed, I believe that the framework that was used as a lens to present the research outlined in this review can also facilitate educators to encourage TESOL teachers to reflect on all aspects of their practice, because it is grounded in the belief that teachers are "whole persons and teaching is multi-dimensional (moral, ethical, aesthetic, nuanced, and complex)" (Klein, 2008: 112). The results of such reflections can be included in a portfolio where each teacher (and teacher educator) outlines how all of these stages have come to make the TESOL teacher who he or she is at that particular moment.

Reflective Questions

- Why do you think that most pre-service and in-service TESOL teachers tended to focus their reflections on practical classroom issues rather than themselves or society outside their classroom?
- Do you think that TESOL teachers should reflect more on their philosophy (i.e., their identity)? If yes, why? If no, why not?
- Do you think that TESOL teachers should engage in more critical reflection? If yes, why? If no, why not?
- Overall, do you think that the TESOL profession engages in critical reflection enough or too much?
- What is your understanding of community-based service learning?
- How would incorporating community-based service learning encourage TESOL teachers to reflect on their identity and beyond their classrooms?
- How can encouraging TESOL teachers to reflect on their philosophy, principles, theory, and practice heighten awareness?
- Do you think that encouraging TESOL teachers to reflect on their philosophy, principles, theory, practice and beyond practice can be a transformative experience for them? If yes, how? If no, why not?

Instruments

In terms of reflective practice instruments (because I discussed this in detail in Chapter 8, I will only summarize the main points here) or tools used to encourage and facilitate reflective practice, results from the review revealed that discussion formats were most popular. This is an interesting finding because it is counter to a recent criticism cited by Mann and Walsh (2013: 292–293) when they said that research on reflective practice is often dominated by written forms of reflection. Indeed, the findings from this review do not support such claims, and if we include the use of online discussions to facilitate reflection (many of which, as Riordan & Murray (2010) pointed out, share resemblance to spoken discourse), we have an even more dominant presence of discussion as a tool for encouraging and facilitating reflective practice in TESOL.

Writing is still a very popular reflective tool used in all types of framework objectives (e.g., see especially the *theory and practice* combination above), and especially by pre-service TESOL teachers. However, many studies reviewed reported that reflection through writing tended to produce descriptive reflections with little or no conceptual or critical reflections. This seems to be what Mann and Walsh (2017) were referring to in their analysis of the problems of having pre-service TESOL teachers in many teacher education programs reflect by writing teaching journals. Indeed, one article offered wise words of caution when both discussion and writing are encouraged to prompt and facilitate reflection as Wharton (2012: 499) observed, when she noted that when reflecting on what they perceived as difficult issues, especially for pre-service TESOL teachers, some use a group format strategically to protect themselves from any difficult issues that arise in their reflections and then "associate these difficult issues with the group rather than with themselves alone" as they attempted to save face with any admissions of weakness in their own personal writing. That writing is used a lot by pre-service TESOL teachers is probably because they do not have a choice, as it may be a required mode of reflection used in many teacher education programs, as a visible record of reflection possibly for the purposes of assessment.

That said, throughout this review there is a noticeable proliferation of the use of online reflections and much through writing to facilitate and encourage reflective practice (especially for the combination for *principles and theory* outlined above) as this has not received much attention in many current discussions of reflective practice in TESOL. Perhaps the results of this review that highlight the growing use of some form of online reflection tools within TESOL, especially through writing, warrant further attention by second language teacher educators and developers so that we can become more aware of how to promote these more effectively to encourage reflective practice at more critical levels. At the very least, as many of the reviewed studies noted, teachers will need some kind of support to help them with their reflections.

Reflective Questions

- What is your preferred reflective practice instrument and why?
- What combination of instruments would you prefer and why?
- Why do you think there is a proliferation of online reflective instruments?
- Why do you think that TESOL teacher education programs favor writing as their preferred reflective practice instrument?

Closing Reflections

I end this appraisal by attempting to address one of the most important questions that has been asked by some scholars in TESOL about the results of engaging in reflective practice: will engaging in reflective practice "improve the quality of teaching" (Borg, 2011a: 220), and will reflection result in "better teacher performance"? (Akbari, 2007: 198). These are difficult (but important) questions to answer, because, when one says "improved quality" or "better performance" for teaching, then do we assume that we have an agreed base line of what "good quality" or "better teacher performance" is in order to make judgments about any improvements to these? Some readers may suggest that this review still leaves open these sticky questions of whether teacher reflection leads to "improved quality of teaching," "greater gains in student learning" and second language acquisition, but as the review was not fully focused on answering these particular questions, perhaps future reviews can fully address these all important issues in more detail.

I should also point out here that reflective practice as I see it not only within the review but also when completed through the lens of the framework for reflecting on practice means that it is or should be embedded in the context of a TESOL teacher's everyday practice as it generates new learning about self, teaching ESOL and student learning in a holistic manner. Thus when TESOL teachers engage in reflective practice, this reflection is not viewed as a tool to "fix" problems perceived or real in one's practice (see also Chapter 2) where teachers are kept down as technicians and consumers of research rather than generators of their own research, as was the case in many of the studies outlined in this book. TESOL teachers are more than technicians implementing what so-called experts, be they academics or publishers, prescribe, where their learning is assessed only by the end products of the tools they use to "fix" problems – a danger within much of the present interest in language teacher research and action research, where such research has been coopted by academics rather than owned by teachers.

Reflective practice is a complex concept and not just another educational bandwagon as some would have us think, as I have pointed out in Chapter 2, and it should be understood in its complete conceptual meaning rather than as a method or tool to "fix" problems in teaching. I believe that TESOL teachers will not be able to "improve" their practice unless they are aware of what that practice entails or what it is they actually do (not what they "think" they do) in and beyond their classrooms. This means a full awareness of their philosophy, principles, theory, practice and beyond practice. With increased awareness and clarity about what we do, we can make transformational decisions about our practice in the hope that we provide more optimum learning conditions for our students. For too long the TESOL profession has been influenced by peddlers of methods that are for the most part teacher-proof and if teachers and students follow these methods, for a price of course, they will successfully learn English.

We have paid a high price over the years in our profession by being overly influenced by these unscrupulous peddlers and publishers (just look at the publishers' exhibits at most TESOL conferences – glossy, digitally prepared books for teaching and learning English, yet few teacher books on how to reflect on teaching English) and others in ancillary fields who continue to try to tell us what to do, how to do it and unfortunately we continue to consume their wares. As a young profession, this is understandable, but as we mature as a profession we are now becoming more aware of the possibilities of teachers becoming front and central as reflective practitioners who decide what is best for their students' needs. Yes, we can learn from *all* the ancillary fields and subjects such as second language acquisition (SLA), sociolinguistics, psycholinguistics, phonetics, linguistics, psychology, education and many more that sometimes seem endless but we *refuse* to be blown off our feet by any one of them. As reflective practitioners we can now begin to shape the TESOL profession to our needs and not allow others to dictate what we *should* be doing.

One thing is clear and that is the results of this review indicate that most TESOL teachers who engage in reflective practice become more aware of their practice and as a result more empowered to provide better opportunities for their students to become successful learners of English. One cannot improve anything unless one is aware of what it is one is doing in the first place. Yes, perhaps this increased level of awareness may lead to an "improved" or "better" teaching, especially if the reflections lead to some definite conclusions that have direct implications for a teacher's classroom practices, but this is not the main reason for engaging in reflection. Indeed, some of the studies reviewed in this book have revealed that more awareness as reflecting on philosophy, principles, theory, practice, and beyond practice can also lead to an affirmation of current practices or no outward changes in teaching behaviors (e.g., Farrell, 2013b), but this, too, can result in an overall better "quality" of teaching.

The results of this review also reveal the global reach of and the robust nature of reflective practice research within the TESOL profession. So perhaps from now on we can as a profession begin to reference *more* studies on reflective practice from *within* the TESOL profession rather than relying on general education studies, as has happened in the past. Of course, as I have pointed out already in this volume, TESOL teachers and teacher educators must be aware of whose traditions they mirror, whatever approach they take, before they engage in or encourage others to engage in reflective practice. I hope the contents of this book have provided some updated information so that TESOL professionals can make more informed choices when making such decisions.

Before I end, I want to point out again that this book has only reviewed 138 studies from various academic journals over the past seven years. Thus I want to clearly state that this review does not claim to be exhaustive or definitive and is only a sampling of the literature over the past seven years as represented in 58 academic journals. It did not for example attempt to focus on emerging trends (although the finding of the review of the growing popularity of online reflections may be considered as one such trend) that could further clarify our understanding of what reflective practice is. I did not include books or book chapters, for example, and this could be viewed as a serious omission, but space was restricted and thus I was constrained from including these. Indeed, recently we have seen the publication of some wonderful such collections of TESOL professionals reflecting on their work in edited books (e.g. Barnard & Ryan, 2017) together with some excellent books exclusively devoted to the topic of reflective practice in TESOL (Steve Mann & Steve Walsh, 2017; Atsuko Watanabe, 2016).

The Bernard and Ryan (2017) collection, for example, contains reflective practice studies of TESOL teachers (pre-service and in-service) on topics such as (collaborative) lesson planning, classroom observation, lesson transcripts, post-lesson discussions, journal writing, reflection on action, reflection in action, critical friends, and focus groups. Steve Mann and Steve Walsh's (2017) excellent book is very relevant to this book in that it outlines an empirical, data-led approach to reflective practice and uses excellent examples of real data along with reflexive vignettes from a range of contexts in order to help teachers to reflect on their practices. Mann and Walsh also note the importance of dialogue as crucial for reflection as is allows for clarification, questioning and enhanced understanding. Atsuko Watanabe (2016) has produced a superb study of the reflective practices of seven in-service TESOL teachers in a high school setting, in Japan. This book can be a blueprint for others (teachers, academics, administrators, government officials) wishing to implement professional development of language teachers in Japan through the concept of reflective practice.

These are only some of the collections that indicate the robust nature of research on the practices that encourage TESOL teachers to reflect. This challenge of including books, book chapters, monographs and the like should be noted in subsequent discussions and analysis of the literature of the practices that encourage TESOL teachers to reflect.

Overall, the review of the research indicates that both pre-service and in-service TESOL teachers are interested in, and feel they benefit from, reflecting on various aspects of their practice. In addition, the positive impact reported in most of these studies on the increased level of awareness that is generated from such reflections seems to provide further opportunities and motivation for TESOL teachers to further explore and in some instances even challenge their current approaches to their practice, especially when they note any tensions between their philosophy, principles, theory and practice both inside and outside the language classroom. Thus in this review that disseminates evidence-based knowledge about reflection, I have attempted to present a general appraisal of these research contributions. I hope the review encourages future language teacher educators and TESOL teachers with all ranges of experience to encourage each other to engage in reflective practice so that ultimately our students benefit from our knowledge of our practices.

Reflective Questions

- What struck you most from the reviews of the various studies on the practices that encourage TESOL teachers to reflect?
- Why do you think it would be important for language teacher educators, when encouraging TESOL teachers to reflect, to understand whose tradition this reflection mirrors?
- In terms of the framework for reflecting on different practice levels/stages (philosophy, principles, theory, practice and beyond practice), which level/stage or stages interest you the most to focus your reflections on and why?
- Why do you think that the focus of much of the research on reflective practice combines principles, theory and practice and not much on philosophy and beyond practice?

- What context are you in and how will this context influence your engaging in reflective practice and why?
- What is your understanding of the idea that TESOL teachers will not be able to "improve" their teaching unless they are aware of what that teaching entails in the first place? Do you agree with this idea?
- Do you think this review still leaves open these sticky questions of whether teacher reflection leads to "improved quality of teaching" or "greater gains in student learning" and second language acquisition? If yes, how do you think we can answer these questions?

Conclusion

In this book I have attempted to review research (138 studies) published over seven years (2009–2015) in academic journals, in which TESOL teachers were encouraged to reflect on their work. After exploring and appraising the different definitions of reflective practice, I presented these studies through the lens of a holistic framework that I have recently developed (Farrell, 2015a), in an effort to provide a clearer means of how the literature can be understood. I choose the framework to present the research as both a "reflective" and a "reflexive" approach to reflective practice and also a response to a recent widely cited criticism of the narrowness of many of the approaches used to encourage reflective practice (regardless of the field of study) that have often viewed reflection and reflective practice solely as a one-dimensional, intellectual exercise, while overlooking the inner life of teachers where reflection can not only lead to awareness of teaching practices but also self-awareness for a more holistic view of reflection and reflective practice

I should point out that one interest for me in writing this book was to present this substantive body of research that exists on reflective practice in TESOL and thus counteract the claims by some scholars that not much research on reflective practice has been conducted on this topic in the field. In addition I do not want to say which study/studies or approaches are better than others as I believe strongly that they are *all* of value to the field of TESOL. I have attempted to provide for TESOL teachers, researchers, scholars, teacher educators, supervisors, administrators and many others one location where all can easily access these studies and decide for themselves which ones they may want to read more about and which are suitable perhaps to replicate in their particular context. No such location has existed before and we in the field of TESOL have been looking outside to other fields for direction on the practices that encourage teachers to reflect. I believe with this book, we no longer have to look outside and we can begin to cite the research more on these practices within the field of TESOL.

REFERENCES

Abednia, A. (2012). Teachers' professional identity: Contributions of a critical EFL teacher education course in Iran. *Teaching and Teacher Education*, 28(5), 706–717.

Abednia, A., Hovassapian, A., Teimournezhad, S., & Ghanbari, N. (2013). Reflective journal writing: Exploring in-service EFL teachers' perceptions. *System*, 41(3), 503–514.

Ahmadi, P., Samad, A. A., & Noordin, N. (2013). Identity formation of TEFL graduate students through oral discourse socialization. *Theory and Practice in Language Studies*, 3(10), 1764–1769.

Akbari, R. (2007). Reflections on reflection: A critical appraisal of reflective practice in L2 teacher education. *System*, 35, 192–207.

Akbari, R., Behzadpoor, F., & Dadvand, B. (2010). Development of English language teaching reflection inventory. *System*, 38(2), 211–227.

Akcan, S. (2010). Watching teacher candidates watch themselves: Reflections on a practicum program in Turkey. *Profile Issues in Teachers Professional Development*, 12(1), 33–45.

Aliakbari, M., & Bazyar, A. (2012). Exploring the impact of parallel teaching on general language proficiency of EFL learners. *Journal of Pan-Pacific Association of Applied Linguistics*, 16(1), 55–71.

Aliakbari, M., & Nejad, A. M. (2013). On the effectiveness of team teaching in promoting learners' grammatical proficiency. *Canadian Journal of Education*, 36(3), 5–22.

Arshavskaya, E., & Whitney, A. E. (2014). Promoting pre-service second language (L2) teacher learning via narrative: A sociocultural perspective. *Journal of Language Teaching & Research*, 5(4), 731–741.

Arslan, F. Y., & Ilin, G. (2013). Effects of peer coaching for the classroom management skills of teachers. *Journal of Theory & Practice in Education (JTPE)*, 9(1), 43–59.

Bai, B. (2014). Enhancing in-service teachers' professional learning through a school-based professional development program in Hong Kong. *Journal of Education for Teaching*, 40(4), 434–436.

Banegas, D., Pavese, A., Velázquez, A., & Vélez, S. M. (2013). Teacher professional development through collaborative action research: Impact on foreign English-language teaching and learning. *Educational Action Research*, 21(2), 185–201.

Barkhuizen, G. (2010). An extended positioning analysis of a pre-service teacher's better life small story. *Applied Linguistics*, 31(2), 282–300.

Barkhuizen, G., & Wette, R. (2008). Narrative frames for investigating the experiences of language teachers. *System*, 36 (3), 372–387.

Barnard, R., & Ryan, J. (Eds.) (2017). *Reflective practice: Voices from the field* (pp. 8–19). New York: Routledge.

Benesch, S. (2012). *Considering emotions in critical English language teaching.* New York: Routledge/Taylor & Francis.

Best, K. (2011). Transformation through research-based reflection: A self-study of written feedback practice. *TESOL Journal*, 2(4), 492–509.

Birbirso, D. T. (2012). Reflective practicum: Experience of the Ethiopian context. *Reflective Practice*, 13(6), 857–869.

Bleakley, A. (1999). From reflective practice to holistic reflexivity. *Studies in Higher Education*, 24, 315–330.

Borg, S. (2011a). The impact of in-service teacher education on language teachers' beliefs. *System*, 39(3), 370–380.

Borg, S. (2011b). Language teacher education. In J. Simpson (Ed.), *The Routledge handbook of applied linguistics* (pp. 215–228). London: Routledge.

Cabaroglu, N. (2014). Professional development through action research: Impact on self-efficacy. *System*, 44(0), 79–88.

Chan, C. (2015). Tensions and complexities in school-university collaboration. *Asia Pacific Journal of Education*, 35(1), 111–124.

Chao, C. (2015). Rethinking transfer: Learning from CALL teacher education as consequential transition. *Language Learning & Technology*, 19(1), 102–118.

Chen, W. (2012). Professional growth during cyber collaboration between pre-service and in-service teachers. *Teaching and Teacher Education: An International Journal of Research and Studies*, 28(2), 218–228.

Chi, F. (2013). Turning experiences into critical reflections: Examples from Taiwanese in-service teachers. *Asia-Pacific Journal of Teacher Education*, 41(1), 28–40.

Chick, M. (2015). The education of language teachers: Instruction or conversation? *ELT Journal*, 69(3), 297–307.

Chien, C. (2013). Analysis of a language teacher's journal of classroom practice as reflective practice. *Reflective Practice*, 14(1), 131–143.

Chik, A., & Breidbach, S. (2011). Online language learning histories exchange: Hong Kong and German perspectives. *TESOL Quarterly*, 45(3), 553–564.

Cirocki, A., Tennekoon, S., & Pena Calvo, A. (2014). Research and reflective practice in the ESL classroom: Voices from Sri Lanka. *Australian Journal of Teacher Education*, 39(4), 2.

Collin, S., Karsenti, T., & Komis, V. (2013). Reflective practice in initial teacher training: Critiques and perspectives. *Reflective Practice*, 14(1), 104–117.

Conway, C., & Denny, H. (2013). Reflection and dialogue on postgraduate professional development for experienced language teachers. *New Zealand Studies in Applied Linguistics*, 19(1), 5–20.

Cornford, I. R. (2002). Reflective teaching: Empirical research findings and some implications for teacher education. *Journal of Vocational Education and Training*, 54(2), 219–236.

Cutrim Schmid, E. (2011). Video-stimulated reflection as a professional development tool in interactive whiteboard research. *Recall*, 23(3), 252–270.

Cutrim Schmid, E., & Hegelheimer, V. (2014). Collaborative research projects in the technology-enhanced language classroom: Pre-service and in-service teachers exchange knowledge about technology. *Recall*, 26(3), 315–332.

Dajani, M. (2015). Preparing Palestinian reflective English language teachers through classroom based action research. *Australian Journal of Teacher Education*, 40(3), 25.

Day, R. R. (2013). Peer observation and reflection in the ELT practicum. *International Journal of Literature and Language Education*, 2013 (52), 1–8.

Deng, L., & Yuen, A. H. K. (2011). Towards a framework for educational affordances of blogs. *Computers & Education*, 56(2), 441–451.

Dewey, J. (1933). *How we think*. Madison, WI: University of Wisconsin Press.

Dooly, M., & Sadler, R. (2013). Filling in the gaps: Linking theory and practice through telecollaboration in teacher education. *Recall*, 25(1), 4–29.

Ecclestone, K. (1996). The reflective practitioner: Mantra or a model for emancipation? *Studies in the Education of Adults*, 28(2), 146–161.

Engin, M. (2015). Written artefacts in post-conference feedback sessions: The running commentary as a support for teacher learning. *Journal of Education for Teaching: International Research and Pedagogy*, 41(3), 254–266.

Erlandson, P. (2006). Giving up the ghost: The control-matrix and reflection-in-action. *Reflective Practice*, 7, 115–124.

Eröz-Tuğa, B. (2012). Reflective feedback sessions using video recordings. *ELT Journal*, 67(2), 175–183.

Fahim, M., Hamidi, H., & Sarem, S. N. (2013). Investigating the role of teachers' self-monitoring in the learners' willingness to communicate: A case of Iranian EFL learners. *Journal of Language Teaching & Research*, 4(3), 624–635.

Farr, F., & Riordan, E. (2012). Students' engagement in reflective tasks: An investigation of interactive and non-interactive discourse corpora. *Classroom Discourse*, 3(2), 129–146.

Farr, F., & Riordan, E. (2015). Tracing the reflective practices of student teachers in online modes. *Recall*, 27(1), 104–123.

Farrell, T. S. C. (1999a). The Reflective assignment: Unlocking pre-service English teachers' beliefs on grammar teaching. *RELC Journal*, 30, 1–17.

Farrell, T. S. C. (1999b). Reflective practice in an EFL teacher development group. *System*, 27(2), 157–172.

Farrell, T. S. C. (2001). Tailoring reflection to individual needs: A TESOL case study. *Journal of Education in Teaching*, 21, 23–38.

Farrell, T. S. C. (2004). *Reflective practice in action*. Thousand Oaks, CA: Corwin Press.

Farrell, T. S. C. (2006). Reflective practice in action: A case study of a writing teacher's reflections on practice. *TESL Canada Journal*, 23(2), 77–90.

Farrell, T. S. C. (2008). *Reflective Language Teaching: From Research to Practice*. London: Continuum.

Farrell, T. S. C. (2011a). "Keeping SCORE": Reflective practice through classroom observations. *RELC Journal*, 42(3), 265–272.

Farrell, T. S. C. (2011b). Exploring the professional role identities of experienced ESL teachers through reflective practice. *System*, 39(1), 54–62.

Farrell, T. S. C. (2012). Exploring the professional role identities of novice ESL teachers through reflective practice. *The European Journal of Applied Linguistics and TESOL*, 1(1), 2–14.

Farrell, T. S. C. (2013a). Critical incident analysis through narrative reflective practice: A case study. *Iranian Journal of Language Teaching Research*, 1(1), 79–89.

Farrell, T. S. C. (2013b). Teacher self-awareness through journal writing. *Reflective Practice*, 14(4), 465–471.

Farrell, T. S. C. (2013c). *Reflective teaching*. Alexandria, VA: TESOL International Publications.

Farrell, T. S. C. (2013d). *Reflective writing for language teachers*. London: Equinox.

Farrell, T. S. C. (2014a). "I feel like I've plateaued professionally … gone a little stale": Mid-career reflections in a teacher discussion group . *Reflective Practice*, 15(4), 504–517.

Farrell, T. S. C. (2014b). *Reflective practice in ESL teacher development groups: From practices to principles*. Basingstoke: Palgrave Macmillan.

Farrell, T. S. C. (2015a). *Promoting teacher reflection in second language education: A framework for TESOL Professionals*. New York: Routledge.

Farrell, T. S. C. (2015b). Reflecting on teacher–student relations in TESOL. *ELT Journal: English Language Teaching Journal*, 69(1), 26–34.

Farrell, T. S. C. (Ed.) (2015c). *International perspectives on English language teacher education: Innovations from the field*. Basingstoke: Palgrave Macmillan.

Farrell, T. S. C. (2016). *From trainee to teacher: Reflective practice for novice teachers*. London: Equinox.

Farrell, T. S. C. (2017). "Who I am is how I teach": Reflecting on teacher role identity. In G. Barkhuizen (Ed.), *Reflections on language teacher identity research* (pp. 183–189). London: Routledge.

Farrell, T. S. C., & Bennis, K. (2013). Reflecting on ESL teacher beliefs and classroom practices: A case study. *RELC Journal*, 44(2), 163–176.

Farrell, T. S. C., & Ives, J. (2015). Exploring teacher beliefs and classroom practices through reflective practice. *Language Teaching Research*, 19(5), 594–610.

Fendler, L. (2003). Teacher reflection in a hall of mirrors: Historical influences and political reverberations. *Educational Researcher*, 32(3), 16–25.

Feng-ming Chi. (2010). Reflection as teaching inquiry: Examples from Taiwanese in-service teachers. *Reflective Practice*, 11(2), 171–183.

Fleming, D., Bangou, F., & Fellus, O. (2011). ESL teacher-candidates' beliefs about language. *TESL Canada Journal*, 29(1), 39–56.

Gan, Z. (2014). Learning from interpersonal interactions during the practicum: A case study of non-native ESL student teachers. *Journal of Education for Teaching*, 40(2), 128–139.

Gao, X., Barkhuizen, G., & Chow, A. (2011). "Nowadays, teachers are relatively obedient": Understanding primary school English teachers' conceptions of and drives for research in China. *Language Teaching Research*, 15(1), 61–81.

Genc, Z. S. (2010). Teacher autonomy through reflective journals among teachers of English as a foreign language in Turkey. *Teacher Development*, 14(3), 397–409.

Golombek, P. R. (2015). Redrawing the boundaries of language teacher cognition: Language teacher educators' emotion, cognition, and activity. *Modern Language Journal*, 99(3), 470–484.

Golombek, P., & Doran, M. (2014). Unifying cognition, emotion, and activity in language teacher professional development. *Teaching and Teacher Education*, 39, 102–111.

Guerrero Nieto, C. H., & Meadows, B. (2015). Global professional identity in deterritorialized spaces: A case study of a critical dialogue between expert and novice nonnative

English speaker teachers (Identidad profesional global en espacios desterritorializados: Un estudio de caso de los diálogos críticos entre profesores de inglés no nativos). *PROFILE: Issues in Teachers' Professional Development*, 17(2), 13–27.

Gun, B. (2010). Quality self-reflection through reflection training. *ELT Journal*, 65(2), 126–135.

Hatton, N., & Smith, D. (1995). Reflection in teacher education: Towards definition and implementation. *Teaching and Teacher Education*, 11, 33–39.

Haugh, M. (2008). The discursive negotiation of international student identities. *Discourse: Studies in the Cultural Politics of Education*, 29(2), 207–222.

He, Y., & Prater, K. (2014). Writing together, learning together: Teacher development through community service learning. *Teachers & Teaching*, 20(1), 32–44.

Hepple, E. (2012). Questioning pedagogies: Hong Kong pre-service teachers' dialogic reflections on a transnational school experience. *Journal of Education for Teaching: International Research and Pedagogy*, 38(3), 309–322.

Hernandez, L. J. (2015). Making sense of SLA theories through reflection. *Lenguaje*, 43(1), 137–158.

Hung, H., & Yeh, H. (2013). Forming a change environment to encourage professional development through a teacher study group. *Teaching & Teacher Education*, 36, 153–165.

Ito, R. (2012). Expansive visibilization to stimulate EFL teacher reflection. *TESL Canada Journal*, 29(2), 74–95.

Johnson, K. E. (2009). *Second language teacher education: A sociocultural perspective.* New York: Routledge.

Johnson, K. E., & Golombek, P. R. (2011). The transformative power of narrative in second language teacher education. *TESOL Quarterly*, 45(3), 486–509.

Kabilan, M. K., Adlina, W. F. W., & Embi, M. A. (2011). Online collaboration of English language teachers for meaningful professional development experiences. *English Teaching: Practice and Critique*, 10(4), 94–115.

Kaneko-Marques, S. (2015). Reflective teacher supervision through videos of classroom teaching (Supervisión colaborativa docente a través de clases grabadas en video). *PROFILE: Issues in Teachers' Professional Development*, 17(2), 63–79.

Kang, Y., & Cheng, X. (2013). Teacher learning in the workplace: A study of the relationship between a novice EFL teacher's classroom practices and cognition development. *Language Teaching Research*, 18(2), 169–186.

Kanno, Y., & Stuart, C. (2011). Learning to become a second language teacher: Identities-in-practice. *The Modern Language Journal*, 95(2), 236–252.

Kaur, K. (2015). The emergent nature of strategic mediation in ESL teacher education. *Language Teaching Research*, 19(3), 374–388.

Kayaoglu, N. M. (2015). Teacher researchers in action research in a heavily centralized education system. *Educational Action Research*, 23(2), 140–161.

Kiely, R., & Davis, M. (2010). From transmission to transformation: Teacher learning in English for speakers of other languages. *Language Teaching Research*, 14(3), 277–295.

Kissau, S. P., & King, E. T. (2015). Peer mentoring second language teachers: A mutually beneficial experience? *Foreign Language Annals*, 48(1), 143–160.

Klein, S. (2008). Holistic reflection in teacher education: Issues and strategies. *Reflective Practice*, 9, 111–121.

Kolb, D. (1984). *Experiential learning as the science of learning and development.* Englewood Cliffs, NJ: Prentice Hall.

Kömür, S. & Çepik, H. (2015). Diaries as a reflective tool in pre-service language teacher education. *Educational Research and Reviews*, 10(12), 1593–1598.

Kong, M. (2014). Shifting sands: A resilient Asian teacher's identity work in Australia. *Asia Pacific Journal of Education*, 34(1), 80–92.

Korthagen, F. (2001). *Linking practice and theory: The pedagogy of realistic teacher education.* Mahwah, NJ: Lawrence Erlbaum Associates.

Korthagen, F. (2010). Situated learning theory and the pedagogy of teacher education: Towards an integrative view of teacher behavior and teacher learning. *Teaching and Teacher Education*, 26, 98–106.

Kozlova, I., & Priven, D. (2015). ESL teacher training in 3D virtual worlds. *Language Learning & Technology*, 19(1), 83–101.

Kumaravadivelu, B. (2012). *Language teacher education for a global society: A modular model for knowing, analyzing, recognizing, doing and seeing.* New York: Routledge.

Lakshmi, B. S. (2012). Reflective practice through video recording and journal writing: A case study. *3L: Language, Linguistics, Literature: The Southeast Asian Journal of English Language Studies*, 18(4), 193–201.

Lakshmi, B. S. (2014). Reflective practice through journal writing and peer observation: A case study. *Turkish Online Journal of Distance Education*, 15(4), 189–204.

Lasagabaster, D., & Sierra, J. M. (2011). Classroom observation: Desirable conditions established by teachers. *European Journal of Teacher Education*, 34(4), 449–463.

Lim, H. (2011). Concept maps of Korean EFL student teachers' autobiographical reflections on their professional identity formation. *Teaching and Teacher Education*, 27(6), 969–981.

Lin, W., Shein, P. P., & Yang, S. C. (2012). Exploring personal EFL teaching metaphors in pre-service teacher education. *English Teaching: Practice and Critique*, 11(1), 183–199.

Liu, Y., & Xu, Y. (2011). Inclusion or exclusion?: A narrative inquiry of a language teacher's identity experience in the "new work order" of competing pedagogies. *Teaching and Teacher Education*, 27(3), 589–597.

Loughran, J.J. (2000). Effective reflective practice. A paper presented at Making a difference through Reflective practices: Values and Actions conference. University College of Worcester, July 2000.

Luo, W. (2014). An exploration of professional development programs for teachers of collaborative teaching of EFL in Taiwan: A case study. *The Asia-Pacific Education Researcher*, 23(3), 403–412.

McLaughlin, T. (1999). Beyond the reflective teacher. *Educational Philosophy and Theory*, 31, 9–25.

McLoughlin, D., & Mynard, J. (2009). An analysis of higher order thinking in online discussions. *Innovations in Education and Teaching International*, 46(2), 147–160.

Mak, B., & Pun, S. (2015). Cultivating a teacher community of practice for sustainable professional development: Beyond planned efforts. *Teachers and Teaching: Theory and Practice*, 21(1), 4–21.

Mak, S. H. (2011). Tensions between conflicting beliefs of an EFL teacher in teaching practice. *RELC Journal*, 42(1), 53–67.

Mann, S., & Walsh, S. (2013). RP or "RIP": A critical perspective on reflective practice. *Applied Linguistics Review*, 4(2), 291–315.

Mann, S., & Walsh, S. (2017). *Reflective practice in English language teaching: Research-based principles and practices.* New York: Routledge.

Marcos, J. M., Sanchez, E., & Tillema, H. H. (2011). Promoting teacher reflection: What is said to be done. *Journal of Education for Teaching*, 37(1), 21–36.

Mercado, L. A., & Baecher, L. (2014). Video-based self-observation as a component of developmental teacher evaluation. *Global Education Review*, 1(3) 69–77.

Min, H. (2013). A case study of an EFL writing teacher's belief and practice about written feedback. *System*, 41(3), 625–638.

Mirici, I. H., & Hergüner, S. (2015). A digital European self-assessment tool for student teachers of foreign languages: The EPOSTL. *Turkish Online Journal of Educational Technology*, 14(1), 1–10.

Mitton-Kükner, J., & Akyüz, Ç. (2012). Burrowing into the reciprocal learning collaboration of two instructors in an English-medium university in Turkey. *Teacher Development*, 16(4), 425–442.

Morgan, B. (2009). Fostering transformative practitioners for critical EAP: Possibilities and challenges. *Journal of English for Academic Purposes*, 8, 86–99.

Morton, T., & Gray, J. (2010). Personal practical knowledge and identity in lesson planning conferences on a pre-service TESOL course. *Language Teaching Research*, 14(3), 297–317.

Moser, J., Harris, J., & Carle, J. (2012). Improving teacher talk through a task-based approach. *ELT Journal*, 66(1), 81–88.

Murugaiah, P., Azman, H., Ya'acob, A., & Thang, S. (2010). Blogging in teacher professional development: Its role in building computer-assisted language teaching skills. *International Journal of Education and Development*, 6(3), 73–87.

Nagamine, T. (2012). A metaphor analysis of preservice EFL teachers' beliefs regarding professional identity. *The Asian EFL Journal*, 14(2) 141–171.

Nguyen, H. T. M. (2013). Peer mentoring: A way forward for supporting preservice EFL teachers psychosocially during the practicum. *Australian Journal of Teacher Education*, 38(7), 30–44.

Nguyen, H. T. M., & Baldauf Jr, R. B. (2010). Effective peer mentoring for EFL pre-service teachers' instructional practicum practice. *The Asian EFL Journal Quarterly Special Issue on English Language Teacher Education and Development*, 12(3), 40–61.

Nishino, T. (2012). Modeling teacher beliefs and practices in context: A multimethods approach. *The Modern Language Journal*, 96(3), 380–399.

Parks, S. (2010). Using a WebCT discussion forum during the TESL practicum: Reflection as social practice. *Canadian Journal of Applied Linguistics / Revue Canadienne De Linguistique Appliquee*, 13(1), 52–70.

Payant, C. (2014). Incorporating video-mediated reflective tasks in MATESOL programs. *TESL Canada Journal*, 31(2), 1–21.

Pennington, M. C., & Richards, J. C. (2016). Teacher identity in language teaching: Integrating personal, contextual and professional factors. *RELC Journal*, 47(1), 5–23.

Phipps, S., & Borg, S. (2009). Exploring tensions between teachers' grammar teaching beliefs and practices. *System*, 37(3), 380–390.

Polat, N. (2010). Pedagogical treatment and change in preservice teacher beliefs: An experimental study. *International Journal of Research*, 49(6), 195–209.

Richards, J. C. & Farrell, T. S. C. (2005). *Professional development for language teachers*. New York: Cambridge University Press.

Richards, J. C. & Lockhart, C. (1994). *Reflective teaching*. New York: Cambridge University Press.

Riordan, E., & Murray, L. (2010). A corpus-based analysis of online synchronous and asynchronous modes of communication within language teacher education. *Classroom Discourse*, 1(2), 181–198.

Riordan, E., & Murray, L. (2012). Sharing and collaborating between an online community of novice teachers: CMC in language teacher education. *Journal of e-Learning and Knowledge Society*, 8(3), 91–103.

Rodgers, C. (2002). Defining reflection: Another look at John Dewey and reflective thinking. *Teachers College Record*, 104(4), 842–866.

Ryder, J. (2012). Promoting reflective practice in continuing education in France. *ELT Journal*, 66(2), 175–183.

Sangani, H. R., & Stelma, J. (2012). Reflective practice in developing world contexts: A general review of literature and a specific consideration of an Iranian experience. *Professional Development in Education*, 38(1), 113–129.

Schön, D. A. (1983). *The reflective practitioner: How professionals think in action*. New York: Basic Books.

Schön, D. A. (1987). *Educating the reflective practitioner: Towards a new design for teaching and learning in the profession*. San Francisco, CA: Jossey-Bass.

Senior, R. (2006). *The experience of language teaching*. New York: Cambridge University Press.

Sharil, W. N. E. H., & Majid, F. A. (2010). Reflecting to benefit: A study on trainee teachers' self-reflection. *International Journal of Learning*, 17(8), 261–272.

Shelley, M., Murphy, L., & White, C. J. (2013). Language teacher development in a narrative frame: The transition from classroom to distance and blended settings. *System*, 41(3), 560–574.

Shi, L., & Yang, L. (2014). A community of practice of teaching English writing in a Chinese university. *System*, 42(0), 133–142.

Shousha, A. I. (2015). Peer observation of teaching and professional development: Teachers' perspectives at the English Language Institute, King Abdulaziz University. *Arab World English Journal*, 6(2), 131–143.

Sowa, P. A. (2009). Understanding our learners and developing reflective practice: Conducting action research with English language learners. *Teaching and Teacher Education: An International Journal of Research and Studies*, 25(8), 1026–1032.

Tan, J. (2013). Dialoguing written reflections to promote self-efficacy in student teachers. *Reflective Practice*, 14(6), 814–824.

Tang, E. (2009). Introduction and development of a blog-based teaching portfolio: A case study in a pre-service teacher education program. *The International Journal of Learning*, 16(8), 89–100.

Tang, E. (2013). The reflective journey of pre-service ESL teachers: An analysis of interactive blog entries. *The Asia-Pacific Education Researcher*, 22(4), 449–457.

Tavil, Z. M. (2014). The effect of self-reflections through electronic journals (e-journals) on the self efficacy of pre-service teachers. *South African Journal of Education*, 34(1), 1–20.

Tinker Sachs, G. M., & Ho, B. (2011). Using cases in EFL/ESL teacher education. *Innovation in Language Learning and Teaching*, 5(3), 273–289.

Thompson, N., & Pascal, J. (2012). Developing critically reflective practice. *Reflective Practice*, 13, 311–325.

Too, W. K. (2013). Facilitating the development of pre-service teachers as reflective learners: A Malaysian experience. *The Language Learning Journal*, 41(2), 161–174.

Trent, J. (2010a). From rigid dichotomy to measured contingency. Hong Kong preservice teachers' discursive construction of identity. *Teaching and Teacher Education: An International Journal of Research and Studies*, 26(4), 906–913.

Trent, J. (2010b). Teacher education as identity construction: Insights from action research. *Journal of Education for Teaching*, 36(2), 153–168.

van Lier, L. (2005). Case study. In E. Hinkel (Ed.), *Handbook of research in second language learning* (pp. 195–208). Mahwah, NJ: Lawrence Erlbaum.

Vo, L. T., & Mai Nguyen, H. T. (2010). Critical friends group for EFL teacher professional development. *ELT Journal*, 64(2), 205–213.

Wach, A. (2015). Promoting pre-service teachers' reflections through a cross-cultural keypal project. *Language Learning & Technology*, 19(1), 34–45.

Wachob, P. (2011). Critical friendship circles: The cultural challenge of cool feedback. *Professional Development in Education*, 37(3), 353–372.

Wan, W., Low, G. D., & Li, M. (2011). From students' and teachers' perspectives: Metaphor analysis of beliefs about EFL teachers' roles. *System*, 39(3), 403–415.

Waring, H. Z. (2013). Two mentor practices that generate teacher reflection without explicit solicitations: Some preliminary considerations. *RELC Journal*, 44(1), 103–119.

Waring, H. Z. (2014). Mentor invitations for reflection in post-observation conferences: Some preliminary considerations. *Applied Linguistics Review*, 5(1), 99–123.

Watanabe, A. (2016). *Reflective practice as professional development experiences of teachers of English in Japan*. Bristol: Multilingual Matters.

Wharton, S. (2012). Presenting a united front: Assessed reflective writing on a group experience. *Reflective Practice*, 13(4), 489–501.

Wu, H., Gao, J., & Zhang, W. (2014). Chinese EFL teachers' social interaction and socio-cognitive presence in synchronous computer-mediated communication. *Language Learning & Technology*, 18(3), 228–254.

Wyatt, M. (2010). One teacher's development as a reflective practitioner. *Asian EFL Journal*, 12(2), 235–261.

Wyatt, M. (2011). Teachers researching their own practice. *ELT Journal*, 65(4), 417–425.

Wyatt, M. (2013). Overcoming low self-efficacy beliefs in teaching English to young learners. *International Journal of Qualitative Studies in Education (QSE)*, 26(2), 238–255.

Xu, H. (2015). The development of teacher autonomy in collaborative lesson preparation: A multiple-case study of EFL teachers in China. *System*, 52(1), 139–148.

Yang, P. (2013). Two heads are better than one: Team teaching in TESOL internship. *Kalbų Studijos*, 23, 113–125.

Yang, S. (2009). Using blogs to enhance critical reflection and community of practice. *Educational Technology & Society*, 12(2), 11–21.

Yesilbursa, A. (2011a). Reflection at the interface of theory and practice: An analysis of pre-service English language teachers' written reflections. *Australian Journal of Teacher Education*, 36(3), 104–116.

Yesilbursa, A. (2011b). Descriptive versus dialogic reflection and positive versus negative stance in the reflective writing of Turkish prospective English language teachers. *Novitas-ROYAL (Research on Youth and Language)*, 5(2), 169–182.

Yu-Chih Sun. (2010). Developing reflective cyber communities in the blogosphere: A case study in Taiwan higher education. *Teaching in Higher Education*, 15(4), 369–381.

Yuan, R., & Lee, I. (2014). Pre-service teachers' changing beliefs in the teaching practicum: Three cases in an EFL context. *System*, 44(1), 1–12.

Yuan, R., & Lee, I. (2015). Action research facilitated by university-school collaboration. *ELT Journal: English Language Teachers Journal*, 69(1), 1–10.

Zhoujing, L. (2012). Collaborative action research: An effective way to promote EFL teacher development. *Journal of Education and Practice*, 3(14), 22–28.

Zhu, H. (2014). Reflective thinking on EFL classroom discourse. *Journal of Language Teaching & Research*, 5(6), 1275–1282.

Zottmann, M. J., Goeze, A., Frank, C., Zentner, U., Fischer, F., & Schrader, J. (2012). Fostering the analytical competency of pre-service teachers in a computer-supported case-based learning environment: A matter of perspective? *Interactive Learning Environments*, 20(6), 513–532.

INDEX

110–11; mirroring 109–10; motivation, autonomy and 125; narrative study 127–8; online discussions 110–11; performance, teacher growth and 119; personal bias 114; post-observation discussions 108–9; written documents in 114–15; post-observation trainer trainee interactions (POTTI) 108–9; problem-solving 111; professional identity development 106; reflection journals 113–14; experience of keeping 116; reflective instruments 105–6; scaffolding 126; self-efficacy 108; self-evaluation 118–19; video-based reflections 118, 119–20; videoconferencing 111; whole-class discussions 106; writing 112–17
intellectualization 26
intelligent action 28
interactive online discussion forums 57
intuitive performance 28
Ito, R. 102–3

Johnson, K.E. 34
Johnson, K.E. and Golombek, P.R. 47–8
journal reflection 12–13
journal writing: class discussion and 116–17; instruments of reflective practice 113–14, 115–16; reflection beyond practice 97; reflective practice 79, 82

Kabilan, M.K., Adlina, W.F.W., and Embi, M.A. 110
Kaneko-Marques, S. 55, 108
Kang, Y. and Cheng, X. 87
Kanno, Y. and Stuart, C. 41, 137
Kaur, K. 90
Kayaoglu, N.M. 126–7
keypals 110–11
Kiely, R. and Davis, M. 74–5
Klein, S. 140
knowledge-in-action 28
knowledge transformation: definitions 18; theory of practice 69
Kolb, D. 34
Kömür, S. and Çepik, H. 79, 114
Kong, M. 40, 44, 46, 136–7
Korthagen, F. 34
Kozlova, I. and Priven, D. 83–4
Kumaravadivelu, B. 43, 49, 60

Lakshmi, B.S. 18, 20, 24, 25, 89
Lasagabaster, D. and Sierra, J.M. 87–8, 120–21, 122

learner component of reflective practice 17, 22
learning-in-practice 41
lesson design, reflection on 71
lesson planning conferences (LPCs) 66
Lim, H. 39
Lin, W., Shein, P.P., and Yang, S.C. 52–3
linguistics 143
Liu, Y. and Xu, Y. 43–4, 45, 137
Loughran, J.J. 1
Luo, W. 72

McLaughlin, T. 1
McLoughlin, D. and Mynard, J. 68
Mak, B. and Pun, S. 89–90, 107–8
Mak, S.H. 54
Mann, S. and Walsh, S. 3, 4, 7, 12, 131, 135, 141, 144–5
Marcos, J.M., Sanchez, E., and Tillema, H.H. 5
mentor feedback 81
Mercado, L.A. and Baecher, L. 87
metacognition 17, 19–20
metaphor analysis: appraisal of research results 137–8; principles of practice 52–3, 58–9
methodology: reflective questions on 135–6; review studies 6–8, 135
Min, H. 59–60
Mirici, I.H. and Hergüner, S. 81–2
mirroring 2, 7, 14, 25, 29, 36, 90, 109–10, 134, 144
Mitton-Kükner, J. and Akyüzb, Ç. 44, 45
mixed-method research 135
moral aspect of practice: reflection beyond practice 95, 98; reflective practice and 17, 22–3
Morgan, B. 137
Morton, T. and Gray, J. 66, 68, 69
Moser, J., Harris, J., and Carle, J. 80
motivation, autonomy and 125
multidimensional aspect of teaching 140; social universe of teacher identity 39–40
Murugaiah, P., Azman, H., Ya'acob, A., and Thang, S. 73

Nagamine, T. 52, 53
narrative frames, construction of 48
narrative studies 127–8
narrative verbalization 48
Nguyen, H.T.M. 84
Nguyen, H.T.M. and Baldauf Jr., R.B. 84
Nishino, T. 70–71

CPSIA information can be obtained
at www.ICGtesting.com
Printed in the USA
FFHW010933090719
53459486-59113FF